ON POLITICAL GOALS

Weil Lectures delivered at
The University of North Carolina
1957

by

Edward Gordon

GEORGE CATLIN

Author of

'The History of the Political Philosophers',

'The Principles of Politics', etc.

ST MARTIN'S PRESS
NEW YORK

To
VERA

c 1957 by George Edward Gordon Catlin
Library of Congress Catalog Card number 57-8591
Printed in Great Britain for
St. Martin's Press Inc.,
103 Park Avenue, New York 17

First published 1957

ON POLITICAL GOALS

PREFACE

This book contains, in an extended version, the Weil Lectures, of 1957, delivered in the University of North Carolina. I wish to place on record my appreciation of the honour done me by the University and the Weil Lectures Committee in extending to me an invitation to lecture, on a list which also includes, among those invited, two Presidents of the United States. It would be difficult for me to express too warmly my appreciation of the courtesy and generosity of the authorities of the distinguished university at Chapel Hill, a beacon of learning in the Deep South. I would express that appreciation (if I may say so) not least for their tolerance and courage in allowing me freely to express views on that racial question which I hold to be so critical for the future of our civilization and its political goals ; but about which I am well aware that my views are not these shared by all in North Carolina. I was, however, made aware that the tradition of one of the greatest of citizens of the Old Dominion, Thomas Jefferson, in maintaining freedom of speech, was maintained no less in the neighbouring State of the Union.

Although it is only a few short months ago since I first wrote the draft of these lectures, already some of those matters which I wrote about in a mood of prophecy, as desirable, have begun to come to pass. The plan for a European Common Market has advanced many steps. Suggestions for adhesion to the Commonwealth have been made by one European State, and for broadening the Free Commonwealth have been made by a Commonwealth Premier. A new Dominion in Africa has been added to the fraternity of the Commonwealth. A Conservative sometime Minister of the Crown has publicly deplored the tying up in Cyprus of almost half of " the total of the British forces in Europe who are defending our own front door ". Mr. Nikita

Khruschev has taken steps both forward and backward in the liberalization of the Russian régime. The President of the United States has reemphasized the need for the effective presentation of a Western idea, an idea indeed of the whole free world, which still too much lacks unanimity. In a few instances I have made amendments to the text. In most cases I have let it stand as originally written. After all, precisely what matters is that the political goals of the West conform to a tradition of values which does not change from year to year. Our task is to make that tradition more articulate and more attractive of passionate belief than it has been in the years of anger, but also of irresolution, that have marked the middle period of this strange century of tyranny and heroism.

I also wish to express my thanks to my publishers, the St. Martin's Press, and to Mr. Lambert Davis, of the University of North Carolina Press for their co-operation in the preparation of these lectures in a form suitable for publication.

LONDON.   G.E.G.C.

CONTENTS

CONTENTS

I

THE PROBLEM STATED

1

IF we allow six thousand years for the period of recorded history, before which stretch the ages of pre-history, and remember that there have always been old men who lived to be a hundred, then we reach the conclusion that only sixty lives of people who might have seen each other stretch from ourselves to the dawn of history. When we reflect upon the mind-baffling number of light-years which alone can attempt to measure the size of the universe, our imagination is crushed. Our sense for the worthwhile is abased, for all 'goals' will be, we say, the same in a thousand years.

We scarcely need the astronomer to tell us, further, of this planet, this absurd, tiny, spinning globe, as a speck of cosmic dust, and the biologist tracing our animal ancestry, creatures of ammonia and marsh phosphorus, Lucifer's Jack-a-lanterns, from the tide-water slime, to complete the work of abasement. The work of Copernicus, who deposed the earth from primacy, of Darwin and Huxley, who deposed man, and of Freud, who ruefully confessed that he deposed reason, will not be undone or simply reversed.

Although, for a while, to the anthropocentric Ptolemaic system, which ranged the stars like angels around this planet Earth, succeeded the egocentric mental climate of the Renaissance, this confidence could not last.

The alchemist, indeed, has now achieved in our own day the transmutation of the elements. But he has proved no Prospero to the earth. A new synthesis of thought, still incomplete, will be required to assimilate these teachings.

Nevertheless, the unconquerable soul lives on, humble but not defeated by the mystery, clad, as protection against the great chill of the universe, by the thin mantle of human civilization and its own piety.

What then is this civilization? In part it is a material matter of the techniques of *homo faber*, man the artisan, and of the power that man holds over matter, above all in this atomic age. It is a power to open new avenues of technical progress, no little of it automatic, such as could give men a frightening leisure to think. It is also a power, like the scorpion's, for humanity to destroy itself. Maybe old archaic enmities, using the anachronistic agencies of sovereign tribal states, may achieve that destruction, perchance in some Armageddon on the plain of Israel, where Jew meets Arab and the eagle meets the bear. Maybe man may sadistically wipe himself from this dust-speck of a planet in the universe, God's universe or godless universe, from sheer boredom with dull leisure.

There is, however, another aspect to civilization beside material power and technique. It is the vehicle of human high culture, of the whole legacy of man and of that grand tradition of values, on which I have commented elsewhere[1], and the preservation and maintenance of which is sometimes just briefly called 'being civilized.'

Some would hold that, even in the darkest moment and when philosophies of scepticism or of materialist devaluation assail us, for which these values are only 'epiphenomenal,' yet belief in these civilized values and active faith in them makes the poor, outnumbered Harlequin, man, and his human experiment, worth while. Indeed some by faith would say that he was hereby vindicated—not set, Promethean, over against the universe but one sentient flower of it, one 'thinking reed' in flower.

[1] *Cf.* my *History of the Political Philosophers* (Allen & Unwin and McGraw Hill 8th impression).

For over two thousand years, of the six thousand of recorded history, since the battles of Marathon and Arbela, when Miltiades fought for freedom, and when Alexander the Macedonian—whose striding figure threw in the East a gigantic shadow as 'the great Iskander'—moved on to the conquest of so vast an empire, Europe has occupied the centre, by arms, laws and culture, of the historic stage. Before then, indeed, by civilization was meant Africa and Asia, the wise land where Pharoah ruled beside the Nile, the Middle Kingdom where the Celestial Emperors held sway even before the dynasty of Han, the lands of Asoka and of 'the Great King' of Persia.

In the Twentieth Century, Asia and Arab Africa are coming back into their own, and their rulers are again coming forward towards the centre of the world stage. To the defeat of the Italians by the Ethiopians at Adowa succeeded the single-handed defeat, *mirabile dictu*, of the Russians by the Japanese—and so on to the symbolic Conference of Asian and African at Bandung. For the first time since Alexander of Macedon and Octavius Augustus (whose name the month of August still commemorates), to-day no purely European Power is among the world's indubitably greatest Powers. Since the Sixteenth Century the Mediterranean cradle of the West has been overshadowed by the rise of Holland and Sweden and England. The process continues. For the moment we see a thing unprecedented: the eclipse of the whole European peninsula itself.

The area of full civilization is far narrower than that of the lands which history describes. Two wars have reminded us that Dark Ages are possible and that this full civilization is a very localised and a very fragile thing. 'High culture' (as distinct from the innumerable local primitive 'cultures' which anthropologists describe) is a rare plant, existing only in a few cultivated portions of good earth on the world's surface. Cynics have even denied its existence north of Birmingham

9

or west of Boston (save in San Francisco alone) or east of Vienna! This is, of course, quite untrue. What we have said of Europe must certainly not be understood as suggesting that, for these two thousand years, all the civilization that mattered (as distinct from the military and industrial power) was a perquisite of 'the West' or of Europe. The Europeans over-estimate themselves.

The great religions of the world are none of them European, however marked the synthesis of one, Christianity, with Greek philosophy and, externally and for a short while, of another, Islam. At a time when the Nordics were gnawing fish on the middens of Denmark or, later, the Normans were committing murder and rapine around Rouen, and the aboriginee black fellow roamed in the wastes of Australia, the Confucian sons of Han were developing a balanced and equable civilization in China and the Lady Murasaki was writing, in Japan, her exquisite story of cultivated romance in *The Story of the Genji* and Sai Shonagon was writing her immortal *Pillow Book*.

What have the sons of the Buddha to learn from Nero or the Sung Emperors from Richard III?

All this said, we must repeat our remark about the rarity of high civilization—and add that not only the martyrdom but the barbarism of man is all too frequent. Man the barbarian indeed is always with us, in each generation to be fought anew. Darwin and Freud have confirmed that for us.

The great Victorians, and their French precursors of the Enlightenment, imagined that this fragility, true of the dark past, thanks to the beneficent and indeed inevitable march of progress could no longer be true of the future. Condorcet would prove right in his *Outline Picture of the Progress of the Human Mind*. The Twentieth Century was ushered in as to be one of "peace, progress and prosperity." It was left for Sir Winston Churchill to speak of "this terrible century," which, a delegate of the United Nations forebodingly recorded, had still half its course to run; this "century of the tyrants," for Aldous Huxley; this, for Walter Lippmann, "dark and barbarous age."

While facing the facts and dangers, we must yet not indulge in self-flagellation. Not only is there room for progress, but there must be progress in civilization and humanity. It becomes the West, no less than the East, to enquire with itself about its own contribution. The progress yet comes, not automatically, but by invention, enterprise, determination, sound judgement and clear views. Locke made clear views the test of his philosophy, in the great epoch of Pope (whose *Essay on Man* bears re-reading) and of Newton. This progress to ends is developed by a sense of direction.

What then is our clear view of the civilization to which we aspire? How shall the values of the past be made yet brighter in the future? *What do we want?*

2

The first comment to make is that there is indeed no such thing, with its demands, as 'Western civilization' or 'Eastern,' 'white' or 'black' civilizations. These are local customs. There is only Civilization. That is the basic contention of all true humanism. The distinction of West and East is quite illegitimate. But, in leading in civilized progress, various nations have to ask themselves what title, if any, they may have to leadership; and what contribution they can make or, on the record, have made. All the rest is hypocrisy, acceptance of which is the homage demanded of impotence by power. Mr E. M. Forster has well developed this issue of the human, catholic and personal, as distinct from the local, national and political, nature of culture. No other than Rabindranath Tagore, internationalist author of the book *Nationalism*, has done the same—as, in his own different way, did the Mahatma Gandhi, one of the greatest and most Christian

11

figures of our age, baptised as Aquinas would have said "by the baptism of desire."

Our needs are in terms of high culture and manners, but they are also in terms of material civilization. They are in terms of ways of life, but also of material standards of living; of technical arrangements, but also of the social or political arrangements which control or order them. And, in this book, we shall be concerned not least with political goals.

The really important issues in politics, affecting the future of the race, are too often those which political parties find divisive and inconvenient, and which party caucuses, organised for the victory of their home team, are reluctant to touch.

Without discussing such flighty matters as the hiving of the over-populated earth and the literal conquest of the stars, the material well-being of mankind is clearly connected with the conservation of irreplaceable natural resources, for which there are as yet no adequate substitutes: the prevention of the steady sinking of the water level; the reduction of soil erosion; the increase of food supply in proportion to population growth or (as Aristotle surprisingly indicated as an entirely proper political activity) the reduction by law of population growth to correspond with available food supply; the relations of peoples and races, thanks to medical advance, in their population growth.

Even if the world food famine which Lord Boyd Orr prophesied has not developed, and even if the problem of food supply is yet not ended but only postponed as the highest authorities such as Mr Colin Clark tell us, with a Danish agriculture the earth could carry six times its present population. Indeed we may describe these issues as Nature's Politics or as the real problems of the political order and of its controls.

At the present time the world's population increases by 37 million persons a year, largely (although the American birth-rate is higher than the Italian) in so-called 'have-not'

12

countries. The over-all European birth-rate has declined, but that of Asia, Africa and South America has, on the last reports, increased. So far as we can judge, the great civilizations of the past seem to have decayed from population sterility, bad taxation systems, lack of discipline in arms and, as with Sybaris, too 'high' or comfortable standards of living for those in control.

The issue indeed of maintaining civilization, despite the test which an esteemed colleague, Carl Becker, once applied in his *Politics and Power*, is not only that of population rates. The Venerable Bede tells us that the provincial Britons failed to repel Pictish and Saxon invaders from lack of military training and sheer cowardice, while the courts of the local kings were voluptuous and corrupt. On the contrary the *Anglo-Saxon Chronicle* records the heroic fights of Arthur and of Alfred as fights against great odds. It is not yet easy for a party politician, unless of the grandest stature, to commend great odds, courage, sweat and tears; nor will his public always endorse him, if he does.

Professor Arnold Toynbee, in his monumental work on the history of civilization, which combines much wisdom with no little speculation, concludes that civilizations decline because of a loss of social unity or cohesion among their members owing to loss of psychological contact between the leading few and the masses, who turn to revolt. This in turn springs from the loss, in the few, of creative power and of faith and indeed, finally, from loss of belief in themselves.

This conclusion singularly accords with Lenin's expert diagnosis of the revolutionary situation, under which one 'vanguard' can replace another leading group. We have either the failure of nerve of the right leadership or the cult, individual or collective, of a degraded leadership.

These issues, although basic for the whole human race (including the West)—of food supply and population; of increase of population outside Europe with medical and

13

economic advance, and of decline within Europe; of regulation of resources without totalitarian regimentation; and of advisory and creative leadership with democratic participation—are not simple problems with straightforward answers such as a man has but to hear in order to understand. Political science, although Bernard Shaw said it was required to save the world, is not an easy science of Jacksonian simplicity. It is an evil error to suppose that it is such or to suppose it to be only an art learned in the city halls of Chicago and New Orleans, Messina or Kansas City. *We can yet isolate certain issues*, where a solution seems to be prerequisite to the untangling of the rest.

This cuts down the problem to manageable proportions. Let us do this. It is urgent for the whole civilized world. It is even more urgent for the West in this phase of crisis.

3

"The *polis* or city-society," said Aristotle, whom centuries referred to *par excellence* as 'The Philosopher', "came into being for the sake of life, and remains in being for the sake of the good life." In brief, its primary concern is security and power, and its secondary concern is welfare and the provision of those values which men demand and expect from their society.

St Thomas Aquinas, who was known as Doctor Angelicus, makes a distinction. The secular sword, unlike the spiritual, is concerned with the corporal coercion of evil-doers. But, beyond this, the secular order has an obligation to provide such external welfare or *means to values* that, thanks to these facilities and this environment, the individual may be aided in attaining his spiritual and personal fulfilment. Which of these two allied views of the political and civil goal is the more exact we shall have occasion to discuss later.

But what, Aristotle also asks, is "the good society"? In the words of the Scottish Catechism, the chief duty and

14

purpose of man is "to glorify God and to serve Him for ever." In an older and briefer terminology, man found his life's justification and happiness in working "to the greater glory of God," and in the realization of rational values.

The rub lies in the fact that there neither has been nor is agreement among all men about what these values are. Maybe Revelation tells us or the Church—but only if we first agree on the Revelation or Church. When we ask ourselves, "What do we want?" we have to abandon hope that the reply will be, not only reasonable, but also unanimous. We have to co-exist with minorities, unless we adopt the technique of the gas-chamber and the slave labour camp.

It is here, when we are discussing political goals, that we are brought to the distinction, popularly if inexactly made, between politics and ethics; or, again, between what we have to discuss in political science and in political philosophy; or, again, between means and ends. Certainly, if we are talking about ultimate goals in what we do want and should want, we have to discuss ethics and philosophy and ends. *But, so long as we are discussing intermediary and interim political goals, means themselves to more ultimate ends, we can discuss what social structure and institutions will be most successful, what scientific techniques most efficient, what means as means may be best.* If, for example, we happen to accept it as justifiable that a Dictator be "cut down to size," how do we do it? This can be the first issue in our task of disentanglement.

Some years ago Professor Lionel Robbins raised, in economics, the question how far the subjective satisfactions that a hungry man got out of a square meal and a connoisseur got out of a work of art were comparable, although of course the sums of money which the one paid for the meal and the other for the *objet d'art* were strictly and quantitatively comparable—whether "five times as much" or "five hundred times as much."

15

Similarly, one way of clearing up this problem of political goals could be to admit that different people in life want very different things but that, nevertheless, these people are constrained to a limited choice and to a large measure of agreement about the 'effective truth,' as Machiavelli said—the actual political and social means—thanks to which any of them could get anything substantial of what they severally wanted. To get anything one wants in the social order one normally must have some freedom, some power, some material means, some control over the caprices of one's neighbours.

Discussion of these kinds of means is precisely the task of political science. To say this is not, of course, to deny that many millions can agree, over and beyond the general political market and apparatus for procuring any satisfactions at all, upon specific demands and particular satisfactions, such as agrarian redistribution or free trade or racial desegregation. Such things, without being almost universal demands, may be great mass demands, although opposed by respective minorities. Already here we are trenching on the issue of the valuation of this or that demand, as distinct from the fact, and of whether people really ought or ought not reasonably and properly to demand them.

What, we may ask, is socially reasonable and proper?

To revert to the, maybe easier, issue of almost universally agreed means to any ends, we see that, whatever a man wants, he also wants to be free to get it. And both saint and sinner want power to attain their ends. And this power, if it cannot achieve direct gratification, usually will spell some measure, perhaps through our systems of rules and laws, of acquiring assurance and exercising control over other interfering men. One great, obvious and dangerous field of such interference with others is corporal force and violence.

Hence most political theorists, throughout the ages, have argued that the prime function of that particular species of

16

social organization which we call the secular state is to keep the Civil Peace and to repress or prevent violence. Even those who have said that the state's function (or the function of other organizations of the social order) should be to promote the welfare of the people, have not usually denied that, among welfares, that of peace was primary for the state. When the magistracy and police are corrupt or overwhelmed, the state is far gone in rottenness. Nor does it matter to me whether I am 'interfered with' by being shot by a native thug or by a foreign soldier. Hence, by 'peace,' is here meant both protection from crime and from foreign enemies. "Give peace in our time." Another necessary welfare would seem to be facilities to acquire that minimum of material goods without which talk of social freedom lacks all substance, and power of protection or security in that minimum when acquired.

Is then Peace the prime political goal, for which we all ask as a requisite means for the substantial achievement of any other social (or even private) ends? This, of course, may mean peace only for ourselves, and not necessarily for the other fellow. It can mean an imperial peace, most convenient to those who hold empire. Or are there any other goals such as Freedom or Justice or Human Dignity or a Higher Standard of Living which we could reasonably think to be prior in claim?

4

There are many kinds of freedom. Against some kinds we ask to be protected, and denounce them as licence. Elsewhere the present writer has argued that freedom, as such and fundamentally, is 'a good thing' and indeed, as the great physiologist Pavlov said, in his *Conditioned Reflexes*, an instinctive demand. Power also, at least of the whole human race, maybe a good thing, although some, such as Archbishop Fénelon and Lord Acton, have argued that it is a bad and corrupting thing or a vulgar taste. Few, however, have been found to condemn peace, at least on their own terms. That we want this is something on which men can so far agree that even Hitler put up banners in Berlin carrying Disraeli's old maxim, 'Peace with Honour.'

We are here speaking of civil peace and not of other kinds such as that described by Spinoza, which would be better called tranquillity. And, although men may disagree about the kind of freedom which they want, they all want civil peace. The only question is: *How to get it?* And yet we may perhaps add: How to get it in a—to us—satisfactory form?

This nostalgia is, however, only one side of the medal. The time comes for most normal human beings (although certainly not for all) when they look forward to retirement, and again later when they are fully willing 'to hand in their cards' on life. This light attachment to life, however, is far more common in the Orient than in the modern Occident. It is recognized and exploited by certain Eastern governments. Prime Minister Chou En-lai is reputed to have said that the conquest of Formosa might cost him three million human beings, but that Communist China could well afford that. They were 'expendable.' For comparable reasons the deliberate 'liquidation,' of which the Petrovs supply the latest documentation, of tens of thousands in the Soviet Union can there be tolerated, without apparent indignation, as an incident of government, whereas in the humanitarian West it would produce the 'liquidation' of that government itself.

In the West even the pacific are not prepared to be passive, and see what kind of peace some automatic government may choose to hand out. The government must show some respect for them as individual persons.

The statement of the British factory worker, a heavy tobacco smoker, on being questioned about the connection between cancer and smoking, that "one has got to die some-

18

time and lung cancer is as good a way as any other" may be held to be unusual—although that of the American sergeant, who rallied his platoon in Korea to attack with the words "you have got to die sometime," was perhaps scarcely less rare.

Vigorous objection to being liquidated on the part of Western man, as distinct possibly from the Buddhist East, is perhaps due, not so much to climatic lassitude in the Orient or even to superior physical health in much of the West, but to a certain activism and individualism which connects with the Occidental versions of the philosophy of the Dignity of Man, as an end in himself and not a totalitarian means to some dictator's view of what he thinks to be good and to the peace that suits him, or to some metaphysic superstition of revolutionaries.

What then is wanted is *not just peace, but a just peace*, qualified by respect for human life, civil liberties and natural rights, and peace qualified by social justice (rendering, as Plato said, to each what is appropriate in his function), even if we have to confess that there is much debate about what these rights and this justice may be. If these rights, connecting with Natural Law, are to be discovered objectively (as I hold) by some kind of psychological investigation into human nature, that investigation is certainly not yet complete. However, the substantial enjoyment of civic liberty is impracticable under conditions of endemic war, always by its nature leading to regulations and new restrictions. Nor can the cake of social welfare profitably be divided according to justice, if most of it has to be spent on warfare and its instruments. To all this, then, peace is a means.

The position, thus, which we reach is that we want peace, but we want it accompanied by some other goods, such as freedom and justice, about the content of which (however shaped by our local customs) there is no little dispute. Alack! we are confronted by something known, in

19

political science, as the law of Political Choice, which indeed is little more than the old nursery maxim that one cannot both eat one's cake and have it, or have one's goods and keep one's cash. We have, should they prove incompatible, and life not prove so obliging as to allow us both peace and freedom or social justice, to make our choice. It is not even vigilance but, in the words of Perikles, courage which is the price of liberty.

It can, of course, be said on the highest authority that "war is now impractical." We can say that the answer to Perikles is that the uncompromising courage of the Athenians in the Peloponnesian War spelled the suicide of Hellas by civil war; and that Europe is in grave danger of committing suicide by civil war too, if indeed it has not, in two Great Wars, already done so. Unlike the view of many in 1938, we can assert that preventive war (without some World Court sanction) is immoral; and, as was sometimes said in 1938, we can assert that all war between major powers means "the end of civilization" and the suicide of the race. We don't want the peace of desolation, death and ashes which Rome gave Carthage.

Technological developments since Hiroshima—when the advent of atomic warfare was announced to Mr Truman under the macabre code message "baby is born"—have re-enforced this lesson, not least (be it added) at the expense of the industrial and free nations of the world, as distinct from those of vast rural and tundra spaces. Taken at face value this would mean that peace is so absolutely valuable that it has clear priority against freedom and justice.

We do indeed come here, unavoidably, to the ultimate philosophical and religious considerations of what uncon-ditional value a man sets on living and how far physical death is to be regarded as unconditional evil. The successful tyrant, in possession of ultimate weapons, has a new grip on us such as he never had before. "Skin for skin," said an ironical Satan in the Book of Job, "what will a man not give for his skin?" The whole disillusioned political philosophy of Thomas Hobbes rests upon the twin suppositions that, in a world of hostilities, man seeks power and that man, before all, is motivated by fear to avoid violent death. Beyond and above this imperative there is nothing. In the last resort then—and we cannot avoid this conclusion—the issue does turn on our philosophy of life and death, our philosophy of 'the Last Things.' Maybe it is the Hungarian youth who have taught, by death, the Twentieth Century how to live.

Were, yet, Hobbes and Satan right? If so, then we can foresee a novel Empire of the New Rome, established in the Kremlin around 1984, providing the world with peace— and the sooner America and Britain, potentially 'disruptive forces', recognize the logic of the material dialectic and accept the inevitable, the better for the world and its peace.

This sour conclusion of logic is usually avoided by taking the other route—by saying that we shall indeed insist upon peace, but *our kind of peace*, a peace which does not present the bitter alternatives or (more exactly) which chooses, as priority, our view of liberty and justice, because *we* shall insist upon a peace which is a peace of both liberty and justice. As President Eisenhower said on June 12th, 1945, speaking in London : " Neither London nor Abilene, sisters under the skin, will sell her birthright for physical safety, nor liberty, for mere existence ". The possible conclusion, in war, we shall avoid, by making war clearly be seen as impracticable, because too costly, by the other side under menace of 'massive retaliation'.

It is true that, if some country, even irrationally, thought war practicable, it might have an advantage over those who thought war impracticable, as well as undesirable. It is true that 'war by mistake' might take place, especially (as before and in 1914) between smaller countries, which could broaden

21

out into global war. But a combination, it is thought, of threat of massive retaliation (if practicable—which some expert journalists such as the Alsops in America tend to deny, as of this present), coupled with sincere efforts towards a *détente* and exploration of peaceful co-existence, can maintain peace for all the world that respects also the principles of freedom and social justice.

Some, of course, would sceptically add that, while the peace of non-resort to military measures is objective and clear, respect for social justice can (if in different ways) be subjectively claimed by both sides, and that nobody has decided just what is meant by 'real freedom.' It is just a matter of actual balance of power. Others, in reply, will allege pessimistically that the capacity for moral indignation was exhausted with the rally against Hitler; and that the love of liberty in its death struggle against tyranny, for example, in Eastern Europe, has unhappily been lost, by a tired and comfort-loving generation, of which the views are emphatically not those of Patrick Henry. They pessimistically detect a prevalence of national decadence, not limited to Vichy France. Even to ask the electorates to pay the costs of maintaining a balance is to ask more than the contemporary frightened world, it is said, may be ready to pay. The heroic virtue of the Hungarian Resistance, following that of the workers of Berlin, has been to put a term to this ignominious and defeatist argument.

5

If, then, the free world, and even the Western part of it, and even the European part of that, cannot get all of what it wants, how can it get a relative security and peace for its own pattern of living in its own area, 'containing' any potential aggressor?

Mr Gladstone indeed campaigned in Britain against the genocidal policy of the Turkish Empire of the Sultans, on the subject of the Armenian massacres. But maybe it is not the concern of sovereign states to interfere in the domestic concerns of other sovereign states, be they Turkey or Germany or Russia. These matters are other people's massacres. Still less are they entitled to interfere and busy-body in the policies of South Africa or Alabama.

The issue is stated to be that of peaceful co-existence of different social systems. What are, then, the prospects here?

Before asking what the West wants as its desirable Political Goals, assuming for the moment that it has any 'public philosophy' at all, we have to attend then to these political means to any ends, of which one of the most general and most generally accepted is the maintenance of the civil peace, internal and external. Here is an agreed function of the state. How are the states of the free world to perform this? In the present stage of technical and military development, and short of a war of conquest to set up a *pax Sovietica* or *pax Atlantica*, before which war the imagination boggles, the issue would seem to be one of ways and means of Peaceful Coexistence of Governments—or is it of Peoples?—perhaps accompanied (as we used to say in the Thirties) by Peaceful Change. What are the chances for this, and what are the conditions?

II

THE CONDITIONS OF CO-EXISTENCE

1

IN a statement on May Day, 1956, in Moscow, Marshal Georgi Zhukov praised 'the Lenin principle of peaceful co-existence of states with different political and social systems.' The Conservative *Evening Standard*, of London, headlined this: 'Now Zhukov says it—Peace is our Policy.' Anyone acquainted with Communist history will be aware that Marx made certain exceptions to his general rule of physical revolution, for example, Britain, Holland and the United States, exceptions afterwards cancelled by Lenin.

During Stalin's life time it was argued, at high levels, that Stalin himself was now an old man, interested in peace, and that the doctrine associated with his name of assuring Communism in at least one country, Russia, was a doctrine in opposition to the Trotskyite interest in world revolution. Stalin himself was the safeguard of peace. This opiate hope perhaps overlooked the old maxim about Antiochus Epiphanes: 'tyrants' fears decrease not, but grow faster with their years.' In the recent words of Sir Anthony Eden: 'with Dictators you always have to pay a higher price later on—for their appetite grows with feeding.' But that Lenin himself believed in, hoped for and based his policy, no less than Trotsky, on world revolution and repudiation of co-existence is beyond dispute.

The Leninist view did not, of course, preclude any tactical manoeuvres whatsoever. In a famous phrase Lenin declared his tactical elasticity when he said that he 'would support Arthur Henderson as a rope supports a hanged man.' In effect, then, Marshal Zhukov's declaration amounted to

24

praising the non-co-existence principle of co-existence. It is the kind of enigmatic utterance favoured by some politicians, since (as witness the *Evening Standard* headline) it produces a very favourable reaction, while saying precisely nothing and leaving the speaker uncommitted. In a certain sense the lion and the lamb 'co-exist,' since they live on the same planet and have got so to live. The real question is of the nature of the symbiosis, and whether the lamb is not merely contributing to the digestive juices of the lion.

In the view of the present writer there are few prospects of lasting peace brighter than that of a Thermidorian accession to power of the Red Army, led, not by the political Bulganin, but by the Marshals who suffered in the days of Marshal Tukhachevsky; and of the great Stalin purges; and carried through at the expense of the Party, represented by Mr. Nikita Khrushchev—although it may be granted that Mr. Khrushchev is a politician less intransigent to negotiate with than Mr. Molotov, 'Old Stone-Bottom,' and his men. It can be precipitated by rising economic and national discontent in satellite countries, since it ever lies in the nature of tyranny to dam the waters of opinion, to suit the regime, until they reach a dangerous artificial height.

Negotiations with the Red Army could be of a stable character because its aims, although not small, are yet limited. The significance of the correspondence between the comrades-in-arms, Generals Eisenhower and Zhukov, is difficult to estimate. However, any Army *coup d'état* or lead is improbable so long as the existing regime is successful, and moves from diplomatic triumphs in the East to like triumphs in the West. For the present the Marshals must be regarded as military men under orders; and it is to be supposed that the ambiguity in Marshal Zhukov's statement is a calculated ambiguity, acting under instructions. What then, dismissing speculations about the 'Beriaization' of Khrushchev, is the attitude of the politicians at present in power in Russia?

In London, in April, 1956, Mr. Khrushchev explained with some frankness to Members of Parliament that the building up of Germany would complete the eclipse of France—the assumption here being that the Adenauer-Schuman plan could be regarded as dead, like E.D.C. since the days of the Mendès-France government—and that the Soviet Union would, at this point, enter into an alliance with Germany, with a negotiation about 'the lost provinces,' ending in the total discomfiture of Britain. America was left out of this exposition.

The mutual policy indeed of Russia and Germany, both before Rapallo and since the Ribbentrop Pact, has always been ambivalent. Under Stalin there was no country which the Soviet Union both more feared and also more respected than Germany. At a given point Stalin decided that Hitler was a real dictator, not a demagogue, and a man really worthy of being treated as an equal. After all, Germany, by sending Lenin into Russia to upset the Western Allies, was the indirect author of the Russian October Revolution. There is, therefore, nothing inherently improbable in Mr. Khrushchev's analysis which, however, supposes a complaisant Germany, willing to negotiate with Moscow, and a stymied United States. What, in effect, Mr. Khrushchev proposes as a settlement is a revival of the Triple Entente, this time directed against Germany and the United States. However startling, such a revival, of course, is a proposal which any student of politics could have seen as on the cards, to be advocated some time or another.

This, however, is not the whole picture. The unimportant Cominform has indeed been disbanded as the more effective Comintern was before it. It does not, however, mean that the Communist Parties of the world are not mature enough to obtain guidance intelligently and to follow it. A 'return to Leninism' offers little encouragement, as the new policy, to those who hope that, in international tactics, Communists will be quiescent. Indeed, on the principle that the heretic is usually disliked more than the total infidel, no sooner had Messrs. Khrushchev and Bulganin returned to Moscow than 'the heat was turned on' the British Labour Party, which the Kremlin frankly tends to dislike more than Conservatives. The latter the Communists regarded as offering no modern and, therefore, enduring alternative to themselves. It was Mr. Bevin rather than Mr. Eden whom Molotov disliked, maybe because Bevin had a better comprehension of his tactics than (as it seemed to that comrade) any more typical representative of the British Foreign Office.

In all these matters the Communist doctrinaire attitude tends to be reinforced by the Russian chauvinist attitude, expressed by the president of the Ukrainian Academy of Sciences, Professor Palladin, who, having described his 'victory' in addressing an Oxford scientific gathering in Russian, not English or French (or Ukrainian), added "this episode showed how important it is never for a moment to yield on points affecting our national honour and dignity; nor must we ever tolerate any kind of toadying to the West."

How then does an active international Communist policy, now called 'Leninist,' fit into the picture of co-existence?

2

In discussing the relations of what is called the Free World (by which we mean more than either Western Europe or the Atlantic West) with the Communist controlled countries, we have to consider four separable issues: (a) relations with Communism in general; (b) with specific Marx-Leninist Communism; (c) with Russian Soviet policy as it is; (d) with Soviet policy as it might be. To put the matter very briefly, about the first and last I am optimistic; about the second and third I am not optimistic.

Many of our difficulties, in this kind of discussion, arise because, despite a gallant little attempt by Mr. John Plamenatz, in his *What is Communism?*, most people have no clear definition in their mind of what they mean by Communism, but only an emotion.

Communism, as a pattern of living in which most goods are possessed in common and so enjoyed, is very old and entirely respectable. There is no ambiguity in the Bible that it was practised by the Early Christian Church. It is to this day practised by monastic communities, which take the vow of personal poverty. It is practised, as a dynamic and most interesting social experiment, in the *Kibbutzim* of Israel, as it once was by various communities in North America.

We might not like it for ourselves, and we can hold to the view that, in modern society, it would be inefficient— although one contemporary trouble, in the case of the Soviet adaptations of the principle, is that it can show itself to be alarmingly efficient. It may be held to involve mental regimentation unless (and even if) self-chosen. But on moral grounds, even if a man is entitled not to be confiscatorily deprived of such fruit of his labour as gives him practical independence in reasonable conduct, no indisputable objection can well be raised by sane men to voluntary Communism. This is the kind of Communism which has been described by Lord Samuel as 'Franciscan'; and the usual charge is that it is too good for average men. It might be well that business clubs and Chambers of Commerce should get this moral issue clear.

Marx-Leninist Communism is a bird of a different feather. There are indeed passages in Marx where this man of the Nineteenth Century (distinguishing himself from the organismic themes of later Fascists) asserts that social organization is fundamentally for the benefit of the individual. And, in an equal society, domination by State rule will wither away.

Nevertheless, although Marx explicitly says that he does not favour equal wages, he does advocate compulsory equalization, normally going beyond that aimed at by modern taxation, which is itself social rather than merely fiscal in policy. The rub, however, of Marxism comes not merely in its revolutionary variant of our customary equalizing policy (which some allege is confiscatory policy) in taxation. After all Henry VIII had no hesitation in confiscating, without compensation, most of the estates of the Church, frequently for the benefit of the ancient nobility of England.

The rub comes in the association of this economic policy with a theory of wholesale State ownership of all means of production (as distinct from public control of vital means), thereby tending to set up an economic Leviathan; in the association with this, especially under Lenin, of a political concentration of power in contempt of what we traditionally have regarded as the natural rights of individuals, in a 'fuller democracy' where one acts first and gets a well-arranged mass support later; and in the association of all three with an educational dogma about the structure of life, history and society.

Marxism, as interpreted by the old German Social Democratic Party, has a constitutional aspect and an evolutionary creed. Marx-Leninism, on the contrary, we may deplore as a ruthless totalitarianism at least of the interim (with no present prospect of the interim ending), a 'Red Fascism,' reinforced by all the coercive force of secular power. Nevertheless many people, while thinking that there is here an almost unbridgable spiritual gulf with any philosophy of freedom, will yet feel that sovereign nations cannot be their brother's keeper; that what happens in the internal affairs of nations, and whether they have 'free elections' or not in choosing 'their' government, is domestic and no outsider's business; and that, however we may deplore it, there is certainly here no occasion for war.

We may indeed, with Mr. Edward Crankshaw in his earlier works, indulge in a little geographical or historical ecology. While not favouring Marx-Leninism in principle, in practice we may see it as absolved from blame either because of the tendency of people in great undefined plains such as those of Russia, (or presumably of Prussia or of the Ganges valley or, under some conditions maybe, of the Middle West) to submit to despotism; or, because the oppressive conditions of the Czardom (or of the Turkish Sultanate and so forth) condoned the establishment of a counter-despotism, which did "so much to raise the living conditions of millions of powerless men, women and children."

It is not clear, indeed, why millions of people should have remained powerless, in Russia any more than in India; or why a more liberal revolution might not have been even more successful—if indeed Kerensky's unfortunate loyalty, against Lenin, to the Western cause (which so very nearly issued, thanks to Lenin, in Western defeat in 1918, as Molotov's despicable pact with Ribbentrop again did in 1939) had not ruined the chances of Kerensky's policy.

Yet, however the situation may have been in the past, despite localized resistance movements in Poland and the Ukraine and even in the streets of Eastern Berlin (which caused some embarrassment to the Unready West), there is no present indication—apart from a few significant student stirrings—that the vast mass of Great Russians do not support, and perhaps with better cause, the Stalinist Byzantine tyranny or the regime of Stalin's successors as enthusiastically as, on the record, the Italian and German vocal masses supported Duce and Fuehrer.

That tyrannies, in infringement of human rights, often have popular origins is an observation as old as Aristotle. By tyranny we mean indeed more than constitutional dictatorship; we mean the police terror that deliberately and of policy infringes the human rights of its opponents, majorities or minorities, as they rest on Natural Law. It is an illusion that tyranny, however vile, cannot be popular with some-body if there are large scale public works and bread, and if the gang-warfare is localized to the ruling few. It will be happily supported in whatever it indicates to its subjects is the route of victory against the foe; and will retain support so long as victory crowns policy and prestige maintains 'face.' The man of courage is yet entitled to pose in the case of tyrants the simple moral question, where human suffering *now* is not to be sophisticated away by the metaphysics of long distances: Do you support them—objectively? Who stands with them at Megiddo? The wise man is known by his choice of enemies. Precisely, here lies the key moral choice of our age, the immediate choice for each elector.

This carries us across to the third issue, of Communism as a peculiarly Russian phenomenon. And, whatever we may think of the Russian 'men of the plains,' somewhat inefficiently oppressed by the corrupt court of the Czar and his foolish wife, the Russian ideological control of contem-porary Communist power-centres, even outside Russia, introduces an additional difficulty, present, urgent and non-academic. The dictatorships of South America, Spain, Yugo-slavia, whether or not actively oppressive, can offer no effective threat to the military or social systems of the United Kingdom or of the United States. The Egyptian ruler is powerless, were it not for outside support, in part the support of the Pan-Arab idea, in part the support of Russia itself.

On the contrary, Russia even under its most inefficient governments has been for four centuries a Great Power, so much feared that one century ago the Crimean War had to be fought to check her. No one was more downright than Marx that the Russian had to be checked by force.

To-day the Soviet Union is not only a Great Power but one of the two Great Powers in the world, busily overhauling America in techniques. It, moreover, lies in the nature of any dictatorship that, to make its own people tolerant of restrictions at home, such as any dictatorship is inclined to impose in order to remain in the saddle, it calls attention to enemies abroad who have to be feared. In the words of no small authority, Adolf Hitler: "The more unified the object of the people's will to fight, the greater will be the magnetic attraction of the movement."

Acceptance of the regime, thanks to a clear view of the class or national enemy (or both), becomes the apparent price of national security. We have had many centuries during which to observe tyrannies. Tyrannies, by their nature, are militaristic and expansive if they can be, to distract attention from their own domestic oppressions. The prime danger with the Soviet Union is that, more almost than any other country, it can be.

This situation, where a revolutionary and totalitarian fanaticism, under what is self-confessed as at least having been a leadership of tough, reactionary ruffians and damnable murderers, is conjoined with the possession of almost immeasurable power, is yet not an inevitable situation. *We can imagine*—and it is our fourth issue—*relations with a Russia of a very different kind.*

In the days of Stalin we were told that the revolutionary dictatorship under Lenin had been replaced by a written Soviet Constitution. President Truman himself discovered in Stalin a really very decent fellow with whom "one could do business"; and a French Minister saluted Mr. Vyshinsky in the United Nations, when that notorious Public Prosecutor died, as a gallant fighter in the workers' cause. Shall we say, as in *Timon of Athens*, "for policy sits above conscience"? To-day, from Russia itself, one hears quite other accounts of the regime of Stalin and of the justice of Vyshinsky. However, the hope is entertained that the succeeding regime, not indeed of the deposed Malenkov and of the executed 'British imperialist spy' Beria, but of Khrushchev, secretary of the Communist Party of the Union, and of Bulganin, who

32

watches the Army on behalf of the Party, will be more liberal. The belief of the present writer is that this liberalisation can indeed take place. *But it will only occur when the fanaticism, as shown in propaganda and education, of the Party is replaced realistically by the directives of a Red Army of limited objectives, whose leaders care for none of these things, or when the Party itself undergoes a radical change in the direction of tolerance and of the empiricism which Lenin attacked and condemned. It is the Marx-Leninist religion itself about which scepticism has to occur.*

It has to be seen as the perilous intoxicant of the people, such as first blinds and then kills, a form of methylated spirits drinking. Nor is this replacement, Revisionism and normalization likely to take place so long as the present regime is conspicuously successful in diplomacy, war and economic development. Should it take place, then the Russian radio and propaganda would lose interest in doctrinaire and provocative criticism of the West and Free World (a moderation which the Free World could reciprocate); and the entirely admirable remarks of the sober Mr. Khrushchev at the Royal Naval College, Greenwich, would hold: that we are all interested in peace, and that we shall make little advance if we only spend our time criticising each other. (Mutual criticism between the various Communist Parties is, however, a very hopeful sign).

Stranger things, of course, have been known than that Mr. Khrushchev, abandoning the very core and gospel of Leninism in world propaganda thanks to the successful and realistic pressure of the Atlantic Powers, and not himself 'dizzy with success,' should execute this change-over himself, assisted by Marshal Bulganin and others. But, even in his cups, he has not yet announced this. Instead he has rather suggested the substitution of the war of ideas for the hot war and even the trade war. The very object of Russian policy is 'face' and *the acquisition of prestige,* which, without a shot fired, can influence neutrals and intimidate citizens and satellites. For this precise reason the Berlin strike of the glorious 17th of June, and the heroism of the Hungarian youth, has repercussions in terms of 'loss of face', immeasurable by ordinary military or economic costs to the Soviet Union. They struck at the prestige of the conquering faith and instilled doubts. As touching trade, Khrushchev's theme at Birmingham was rather represented by his listeners as being "give us the tools and we will finish you off"—and "bury you", as he later said.

3

There is no particle of reason to suppose that the present rulers of Russia want immediate war. Patient men, they have not got the neurotic urgency of Hitler or his conviction that, if a war was to come, it had better come before he was fifty or died of cancer. The Soviet leaders can bide their time. There lies the danger, greater than from the paranoiac urgency of Hitler, for well-meaning, comfortable and indolent democracies, which thrive on 'normalcy'. For a generation the Soviet policy, while maintaining domestic morale by up-lifting and hate-breeding propaganda, has been to seek to obtain a breathing space of peace during which they could advance first in the technical race, and then in the race of economic mass production, as against the United States.

In an influential book, *Modern Arms and Free Men*, Dr. Vannevar Bush, chairman of the wartime American National Defence Research Committee, writes: "The weakness of the Communist state resides in its rigidity, in the fact that it cannot tolerate heresy, and in the fact that it cannot allow its iron curtain to be fully penetrated . . . All these things, vital to totalitarianism whether left or right, are fatal to true progress in fundamental science. They are not nearly so fatal to the application of science, but they are a severe deterrent to even the healthy growth of this along novel lines." In brief, before long political control of pure science would make Russia technically backward. It were pleasant if all this were so and these not merely comfortable, opiate words.

Dr. Bush, above all, must know that such is the international character of science that a quite singularly large amount of up-to-date scientific information does in fact reach Moscow. The British scientists of Harwell were shocked to discover how much of what they themselves had listed as top-secret they were being nonchalantly told by visiting Russians.

A weakness in the West is the comfortable tendency to assume that the Slavs are an incompetent race and the Russians, even the Russian scientists, merely a collection of lightly veneered *moujiks*, instead of highly intelligent and imaginative countrymen of Dostoievsky and of Molotov's kinsman, Scriabin. One of the most ironic instances of this *hauteur* was the naive assumption of a sometime Director of the London School of Economics, an administrator during the Allied occupation of parts of Revolutionary Russia, Sir Halford Mackinder, in his *Democratic Ideals and Reality*, that the vital 'heartland' of the world, from Mongolia to Bohemia, which holds the strategic control of the globe, might, to give world domination, be occupied by the Germans. That it could be occupied by the Russians he dismisses as outside serious consideration. How wrong he was.

Dr. Vannevar Bush's conclusions about the strategic advantages of democracy would seem largely to be based upon the actual defeat of the German National Socialists, while ignoring how very near indeed they came to victory. If democratic criticism aids scientific advance, so does highly organized cooperation; the direction without consideration of private profit of young men into scientific studies and governmental institutions; the intoxication of a common cause where (as with Hitler) "all march shoulder

35

to shoulder"; the clearing of all lines so that the grand advance may go through; and the dictatorial capacity for instant action, without 'democratic committeeism' (to use Lenin's phrase), where the common interest may seem to be involved.

Not only, in fact, do the scientists of the Soviet dictatorship seem to be capable of overhauling those of the democratic West. They are actually doing it.

The results are showing clear. The chief of the United States Strategic Air Command, General LeMay (endorsing in almost the same words an earlier statement made in London by the Supreme Commander of NATO forces) in 1956 has stated that, by 1958-60, the Soviet Union "will have a greater striking power than we will have in the time period under our present plans and programs," whereas in 1951 "we could have won a war without the country receiving comparatively serious damage." The crucial years, I wrote in 1943, would seem to be around 1963. (Incidentally, in so far as this is so, any damage to Anglo-American relations at this time increases the danger of the gamble of war; and anyone doing this damage can truly be described as a saboteur, war provoker and player of the Bolshevik game.)

Time is not—repeat 'not'—necessarily on the side of the West or of the free world and its democracies. An uncompromising and unqualified insistence on peace is not—repeat, 'not'—necessarily and at all times in the best interests of the defence of freedom and national security. Such caution and such insistence may indeed well be wise and right, but it has to be emphasized that statesmanship here is dealing with 'a calculated risk.'

In his book, *Peaceful Coexistence*, Mr. Andrew Rothstein, sometime scholar of Balliol and on the staff of Tass, has striven to show that the U.S.S.R. has never proposed preventive war, however odd its conduct from a Western point of view in 1917 and 1939. That the West, including the

United States, did not resort to it when it certainly had the chance may equally be taken as a practical indication of the fundamentally peaceful intentions of its representatives and elected rulers. The 'risk' has been seen and, for the sake of peace, accepted.

How great is the risk is a matter of highly technical controversy among experts. Until recently, indeed, it was held that, if not militarily, then at least economically in terms of raw materials such as iron, time was always on the side of the West to deliver the final blow.

Apart from a proper distinction between potential supplies and supplies actually available, this economic argument must be accepted with grave caution. A survey of the geo-politics and strategy of the crude oil supply would give little support to it. The almost inexhaustible oil wells of the world lie in Arabia or near the Russian border, not in Staffordshire or even Texas. For the moment the Soviet Union may be warned off the essential oilfields of the West. But such warning remains a *matter of power*, in which one cannot afford to hear 'check' and 'check-mate,' *Sheik-me'at*. How grave indeed could such a cry be in Bahrein. How important it is to know the hopes and aspirations of the Arab, as well as the limits of his power.

What dominates politics is not alone arms or (as Clemenceau sardonically remarked) generals—"war is too important a matter to be left to generals." It is ideas and the education of the minds of men—even if men in arms, as was found in China. This is called the shaping of opinion. As Hume said, even tyrannies fear it. Nevertheless in politics there is yet no substitute for power. However, it may be subject to policy, ideas, choice. Power gives the means. And as Napoleon (who knew at Waterloo) said: 'Power is never ridiculous.' It is merely dangerous. What matters is wisdom in its use.

To the cold eyes of the political scientist democracy and dictatorship have certain distinguishing characteristics, certain advantages and certain disadvantages. It is broadly true that democracies are peace-loving in temperament whereas dictatorships, being repressive and politically unstable, have to conjure up fears of domestic or foreign foes in order to rally support for what would otherwise be insupportable behaviour. On the other hand, that democracies are not temperamentally pacifist is shown by their willingness to pursue through, to unconditional surrender, wars that are going well; and their extreme unwillingness to switch alliances and march along with the foes of yester-year—which a constitutional despotism such as that of Frederick the Great, or a dictatorship such as that of Stalin, turning on and off the controlled propaganda tap, can accomplish with ease. They are too easily pacifist in the years of peace and too self-righteously bellicose in the years that follow war.

In a democracy one has to persuade Tom Smith (who may come from Missouri and "want to be shown") to "see the reason why," whereas a dictator can scrutinise with calculation the moves in the chess game of power. What is true is that Tom Smith is normally reluctant—unless it is a matter of a professional army fighting, or of sporting wars somewhere overseas—to engage upon all the discomforts of war when he would much prefer to be told that business can continue as usual. Moreover it must be a very bold democratic politician, unless avid for suicide, who will continue to tell him what he does not want to hear.

We may, then, say that the statesmen of the free and democratic countries of the world have to-day the clearest and most imperative popular mandate, on peril of political death, to keep the peace, at least where major Powers, and not just human small fry, are concerned. Not unnaturally it is held that, if a locomotive driver is involved in a train smash, he will be brought up before a court of enquiry or even before a jury on a charge of manslaughter. He will not be awarded a peerage, as once were the statesmen, as compensation for wounded feelings. To-day the time is now past when Sir Edward Grey, on the key issue of foreign policy, scarcely consulted anyone save his Prime Minister. In his *War Memoirs*, David Lloyd George—here confirmed by Sir Winston Churchill, in *World Crisis*, wrote:

"In looking back upon the incidents of these few eventful days one feels like recalling a nightmare, and after reading most of the literature explaining why the nations went to war, and who was responsible, the impression left on my mind is one of utter chaos, confusion, feebleness and futility, especially of a stubborn refusal to look at the rapidly approaching cataclysm. The nations backed their machinery over the precipice."

Public opinion, in that free world where alone this opinion has influence, would be intolerant of a like irresponsibility to-day. The mandate of the West to statesmen and professional diplomats is to effect peaceful change, to find a peaceful way out. It is up to them as the specialists . . . Within the ambit defined by that mandate to-day President Eisenhower and, even more, the British Government move.

The position of the Soviet Union, and of the countries which it controls by the interlocking ramifications of the Communist Parties, is different. We may repeat that these countries, with the possible exception of Communist China, do not, on the evidence, want war. If they felt inclined to war, it holds true that these rural countries, despite the strategic advantage of their widely distributed industries, can be "deterred from going to war by a realistic appreciation of the massive and overwhelming retaliation which they would bring upon themselves." What rather may be anticipated is a continuation of a political and propaganda policy so successful, in adding to prestige and 'face,' that there is no reason for abandoning it; and an economic build-up at home such that revolutionary changes, for example, placing minorities in power in Italy or Indonesia or *coups d'état* in

39

Singapore or Arabia, could be embarked upon with impunity.

As country by country fell to pro-Soviet infiltration, did any Western country protest, its diplomatic protests could be ignored. Did the West, collectively or individually, then threaten war, these urban countries, with their highly concentrated industries, could be, first, denounced as 'warmongers' and, then, "deterred from going to war by a realistic appreciation of the massive and overwhelming retaliation which they would bring upon themselves . . ." To such a threat a democratic and life-respecting public opinion would be more likely to respond, in protests against the carnage, than a controlled opinion. And, whereas a NATO organization might be strengthened by fear of Russia at a stage when it, by combination, held the final cards and ultimate weapons, such a NATO organization could, at a later stage (as in 1939, with the smaller lands) break up as the fear became deeper, and as each country individually sought to avoid its threatened fate. Indeed such a process seems to be underway now with NATO, concurrently with a 'softening-up' which explains Icelandic opinion, unconcerned for 'the great international routes of communication' until after events in Budapest. NATO is a very incomplete alliance, its limits awkwardly running athwart the Commonwealth, and not even including the whole of Eastern Mediterranean policy within its ambit. However, Russian hostility to it is profound, and I shall not disagree with Mr. St. Laurent, of Canada, that NATO has contributed to the liberation of Eastern Europe by showing that the West has some spine. It would seem then that the Soviet Union is not so much in the position of being obligated to avoid war, as in the position of finding that it *may still attain its ends in victory by other means of politics, economics and propaganda.*

4

No reasonable man, it can be said, will object to Communism, in the general and original sense of that word, as a possible economic system. It will not mean that all will be atheists, any more than is the Russian Orthodox Church, however contemptibly politically gutless or erroneously 'other worldly'; or that all will be any more 'materialist' than they already are. That war, arms and explosives should settle such issues will appear both sinful and ridiculous.

Nor will Communism be regarded only as Utopian. The difficulty rather with all future economic systems, including those called capitalist, at least as touching heavy industries, will be to find any function in them for the individual crafts-man at all. The best that can be hoped will be that, with the increase under automation of leisure hours, some place will be found for individuality of behaviour, for example per-chance among women in increasing numbers returning, part-time, to their own homes and, above all, in variety in education.

The Russian people will be universally recognized for what they are, a pleasant and sentimental people, if peasant-shrewd when sober, excellently described in their virtues and drunken Tartar vices by Leo Tolstoi. Following the advice of Mr. George Kennan, the peoples of the satellite countries will have come to recognize that Marx-Leninist Communism has come to stay, just as once it was thought that in Italy Fascism had come to say, although (by a rather surprising paradox) Leninism, with the passage of time, would be 'liberalized.'

Many are indeed likely to continue to find Marx-Leninism, with its concentration of power and repudiation of individual rights, to be distasteful and to desire a system of free elections. Trades unionists may dislike the system of state control of the unions, speed-up in the factories and directed labour. But this, the cynic may say, will be an individual taste, certainly not a fighting matter, and something about which outsiders from another country will have the tolerance not to interfere. It will be thought barbaric and also ridiculous that these matters should be settled by arms, and indeed by human vaporization. Great Powers may knock around smaller fellows, such as Egypt or Cyprus, who cannot effectively fight back, but will scarcely take on each other.

The mood rather will be like that in the peaceful Hanoverian period in Britain, of reaction against the fevers of the Seventeenth Century and the devastating Wars of Religion. All these things may be . . . In France there has been discussion recently of what has been called the Great Cowardice, but this, probably a slander on France itself, surely does not apply to other countries. Rather they can congratulate themselves on escaping from the infinite devastation and immoralism of total war, and of pursuing a policy of peace, dominated in temper by the mood of common sense. This, then, can be the argument.

Should, of course, war actually break out, it would be suicide, it may be said, for countries on the firing line in Western Europe to get involved. If the United States opposed the increase of Soviet power and war broke out on the issue, for at least months (if not the longer period required by America herself in two wars) all that Western Europe could give would be "all aid short of war"—unless indeed, for example, the neutrality of Canada, the 'Pearl Harbour' of our present situation, were involved. But statesmanship will consist in avoiding such a war.

There is only one major difficulty in the way of this sensible aspiration. Let us suppose that Russia, successful beyond all expectations of five years ago in her policy, saw no reason to abandon her traditional messianic sense of world mission, reinforced by the Leninist world program. Let us even suppose that she saw no reason to liberalize, in a 'bourgeois democratic' or 'natural rights' sense, her present successful regime, which has corrected the excesses of Stalinism by reverting to a more orthodox but even fiercer Leninism. Let us imagine that she proposed to impose, not Communist manners, but some satellite version of Kremlinism upon us . . . or upon, not only East Germany and Hungary, but West Germany and Italy.

Would we then all become Communists, even in the American Middle West, in order to accelerate world pacification? What would be our attitude to a world tyranny that offered peace? Would part of the West even consider abandoning neutrality and joining in a united popular front in order to attack America and speed matters up? Or would we contemplate Resistance, even on behalf of a world which had hitherto displayed an entire inability, even a contemptible inability, to know its own mind?

III

THE BATTLE FOR THE MINDS
OF MEN

1

THE fundamental issue before us to-day is the choice between the Soviet Marx-Leninist philosophy, on the one hand, and the Anglo-Saxon and the Christian-Judaic-Hellenic philosophy of life, imperfectly synthesized although these latter are. It is true that there is something of the Judaic philosophy of judgement and apocalypse of the New Jerusalem in Marx. But there is little of Hellenic light or Christian love, and less of Anglo-Saxon pragmatic moderation.

If our immediate objective is peace, although in a fashion that enables us to display our own patterns of liberty and justice, and if such *peace depends upon some formula of social coexistence which does not merely spell the quiet subversion of these patterns by ideas, not arms, until it is too late to draw back*, then an essential defence is a clear choice in ideas and, through education, a clear recognition of what each choice in direction will involve.

Apart from the difference in social consequence between an architypal example of charity, as in Christ, and a dogmatic faith in class victory as norm of ethical conduct, a major difficulty in handling Marx-Leninism is its intransigence and unwillingness to examine new explorations of old Marxist social-theologies (by which I mean the dogmatic faith or—if *religio* be a discipline—religion of Dialectical Materialism and class crusade.)

In 1934, in my *Preface to Action*, I suggested that Leninist

Communism was a religion—although, like that of the peaceful Buddha, professedly atheistic—only comparable in its onslaught on the West to the fighting faith of Islam in the days of the Caliph Omar. If, instead of Marxist fanaticism, there were substituted a clear admission that Lenin lies in the past, a tolerant admission that there was much to be learned from those of non-Marxist faith, not only technically—as Lenin did admit—but socially and culturally, philosophically and doctrinally, an immense advance to lasting peace could be made. Instead we have fanatical, anti-scientific and angry belief in an infallible creed, conjoined with secular and imperial power, readiness to coerce and unwillingness to tolerate any organized deviation or opposition. Here is the core of alarm. Here is the block to advance.

Materially it should not be difficult to prove to the Western wage-earner of the 'have' countries that he has nothing at all to gain did the international Communist Party come into power tomorrow, to regulate his trade unions, hours and speed of work. Some fascist activists indeed see in the Communist ruthless oligarchic discipline of labour an attraction. Here is the final duping of all the workers all the time, with 'jam to-morrow and no jam to-day' (except for 'the vanguard,' among whom the activists naturally include themselves). Hence in many countries recruits have flowed easily between the two anti-liberal camps and manual workers have flowed, as refugees, away from the areas of 'the Dictatorship of the Proletariat.'

But to the peasant and coolie in even the free countries of the East, the 'have-not' countries, Communism, joined with anti-imperialism and anti-colonialism, can make, has made and will make an immense appeal. For it may well be that it is not so much in Europe, even in Eastern Europe, with developed natural traditions, but in Asia, with so little to lose and a past tradition of centralized despotism, that the major danger lies of the spread of the Bolshevik political pattern. For India itself the pragmatic test could be that of the economic results of parliamentary democracy as against Bolshevism (a more exact word than the innocuous 'Communism' such as we see in Israel), and not one of choice of liberal principles in politics. Nevertheless, these ideas, especially of free nationalism, play their role—not automatically in favour of the West. Indeed the British Empire, not to speak of the French and Dutch, whatever capitalist benefits it may incidentally once have conferred, even for the advantage of its own trade, may seem to dispossessed men no better in kind than the empires of Hapsburg, and Romanov and Hohenzollern, no better indeed, in their eyes, than the old native despotisms. (The Hapsburgs, holding together the Danubian economy in an empire entirely of the European family, may even seem wise by comparison). Here the Americans have, historically, a comparatively clear record, although by no means pure or in a position to be 'holier than thou.'

Communism can appeal to the coolie in Malaya, who has himself no private property, never had, and has no prospects under London-controlled companies of acquiring it, by showing him—however illusorily—the prospect of becoming the owner of his own rubber tree and his own soil. "Land, electricity and power to the Soviets" promised that most formidable of propagandists, Lenin. The material appeal, for countries of traditional despotism, as of the moment is by no means solely in the hands of the Western section of the Free World—not least since much of its 'aid' is passed through the hands of bureaucratic governments and of speculative industrialists and, in some cases, never indeed reaches the common folk.

M. Guy Mollet, in his forceful speech of April, 1956, had much justification for his fierce denunciation of the unimaginative and unsympathetic 'semi-Marxism' of a few unfortunate agents appointed to handle Marshall Aid and the later organisations of this general type, often with half-baked notions that industrialization over-night is "a good thing"; with their philosophy that mere 'production' is a good thing, whatever the cultural consequences, e.g. in a rural, Buddhist country such as Burma; and with their Occidental patronizing attitude and their latent notion that gratitude should be automatic, mechanically following from dollar bounties, bounties pumping up gratitude *ex opere operato*.

Such a view is arrogance. M. Mollet had justification for his Gallic denunciation of offensive patronage by little American bureaucrats-of-largesse, modern variants of the 'milord Englishmen,' and of plutocratic benevolences to inferiors, such as arouse not gratitude but humiliation, envy and hate. In the words of Professor Herbert Kubly, in *Stranger in Italy:* "Dollars and bullets do not win trust. You spend your billions selling yourselves, but very little making friends."

Love is not for sale, even without political strings. Better be poor. Better the comradely aid of the Soviet Eur-Asiatic Union which Lenin himself had called a bankrupt, broken-down country—like others in Asia. If Russia was once bankrupt, it was yet in the same boat as a partner with the rest of Asia, a partner in hope and in suffering, not like an English milord or a Yankee capitalist or a Western European 'lackey.' That Russia had once been and, in terms of recent expansion, still is a great imperialist and colonial Power, although expanding overland and not overseas, can be forgotten at a distance by people whose memory of Western trading imperialism is very recent.

Spiritually, the affair at first glance is in little better case. The Free World has an excellent cause, badly handled. The outraged and generous Anglo-Saxon may claim that he is malignantly misunderstood, thanks to the malice of Bolshevik propaganda. He has virtues of spirit and ideals which are not appreciated. But, then, he does not command, even among his own spokesmen, unanimity of explanation, unanimity of publicity, information, propaganda, to explain just what these virtues may be. He is too lazy a materialist, too facile a pragmatist, to explain. 'When he thinks, he thinks he is ill'; and prefers just to go among Eastern peoples to explain to them better methods of breeding goats and swine. He is distressed when he is told by men, converted to a new religion, that he is not wanted.

Doubtless there is a common social faith of the Free World, although scarcely what Mazzini would have called a religion. A religion of freedom can blaze up in the adolescents, the youth of Hungary and Poland. But does the Anglo-Saxon, the Westerner, himself believe in it ? Has he what Walter Lippmann calls any 'public philosophy' ? And, if he does not believe in it himself or is just drifting, concerned actually only with business success for himself or (as Brooks Adams said should be the American gospel) with power, why should any other member of the Free World believe in him—or any member of the Soviet world of the gospel of Marx yield to him?

In the neo-Darwinian world indeed—and with neo-Darwinianism much of American philosophy, like Marxism itself, has in fact been corrupted—why worry about this talk of the American pattern of 'life, liberty and the pursuit of happiness'? If the issue is the Darwinian one of power to survive, and of material facilities for success and happiness, then this power may be said now to lie—whatever may be the case with 'eternal virtues,' which the American philosophers so often themselves reject—upon the other, or Soviet, side. "Let us be rid," it may be argued, "of this hypocrisy: the issue is just one of power-politics."

'Why,' it may be asked, 'let the Americans obstruct the Popular Front and the peace of the world?' What is 'rotten in the state of Denmark' would seem to lie, not in the crisp gospel of Communism and sacrifice, but on the Transatlantic materialist shore. Is not the *mystique* of Dialectical Communism, or even of the Russian Orthodox Church, better? It is indeed a pretty pickle.

2

Here is an issue of ideas and of those fundamental philosophies of life which do indeed underlie any propaganda worthy of the name, and above the level of what is called 'psychological warfare.' It is an issue of those fundamental views which shape men's convictions, ideas and choices. It is very easy to talk of 'the Philosophy of the Free World.' Let us see just what all this adds up to—and indeed whether the philosophy exists in the fashion supposed.

It is not difficult to say that the Free World (which is more than the West and still more than Western Europe) *ought* "to state its case." This is the theme of at least a dozen books. It is still more important to proceed to state it, and to agree upon what should be stated. The time for talk about "what we ought to do" is over. Let us do it. If indeed the prospect of a 'hot' war is at an end for the present —I say 'at the present,' because there is no agreement about how to keep the peace, founded rather on fear than on accord, did 'the cult of the individual' renew itself with another Stalin or Hitler—and if the 'cold' war has changed its shape, since the Soviet Union is going to be concerned even more with building up its immense economic strength, then where lie the issues?

In a speech in May, 1956, M. Mendès-France said that by cutting a million men from her army, Russia had vastly increased her economic potential—but for reasons not solely economic—and that was her new weapon. "It is ridiculous to think that we are entering a world of simple polite economic competition. *The contest is on for influence*

49

in the undeveloped areas in the world."

If the propaganda campaigns alike of Russia and of the various national Communist Parties are not abated, then it is precisely 'the war of ideas,' which produces changes of conviction, of support, of influence, which remains to be waged. At least this 'war' must be waged by those who dislike the alternative that, within fifty years, the whole world may well be Leninist, and that peace, as *pax Sovietica*, will really be maintained by coexistence on the basis of co-operation with the will of the Kremlin.

Nor would it be difficult to make out a case for the latter . . . Let us pause for a moment to see whither this line of thought would lead us. A writer who has (like Professor Arnold Toynbee) perhaps had more influence in America than in Britain, Professor H. J. Laski, maintained the position, at various times and in divers manners hostile to any clear-cut presentation of an antithesis of ideas, that although violence, silencing reason, was to be deplored, nevertheless all history indicated that reactionaries were likely to resort to force rather than surrender power. To tell the truth, Mr. P. A. Ryan's story of the sedition in connection with the Curragh mutiny, publicly condoned in quarters that should have known better, both Protestant and Conservative, and the training in Ulster of armed men for revolt, gives Laski's estimate, two decades and more ago, an excuse.

The pessimistic sociological estimate of Marx, which puts it into peculiar antithesis to the distinctive Christian estimate of human probabilities, was therefore, in Laski's view, right in effect. The legal position of reformers would then be to obtain a popular mandate and to thrust, as in Spain, the responsibility upon the Opposition of illegally challenging a constitutional, i.e. legally elected, government, however much that government itself might modify the conventions and morality of the constitution.

In so far, of course, as this position visualized the high probability—confirmed in Laski's view by all history, even if deplorable, and therefore to be expected and planned for—of a revolutionary situation, this position can rather be described as revolutionary Menshevism. The theme is more exactly this than it was that 'constitutional Marxism,' with its materialistic dialectic, which was dear to the old (if not to the present) German Social Democratic Party.

However, if we are going to take the step of accepting a physically revolutionary situation—I am not talking, with some members of the Independent Labour Party of Britain, of a 'psychologically revolutionary situation'—as of such high probability as to verge on the inevitable, then it would seem to be perhaps a subsidiary matter how far constitutional forms are to be maintained, provided (as the Bolsheviks urged) that there is popular confirmation *ex post facto*, which could record itself in a massive 99% vote. The real issue, the revolution achieved and established, would rather seem to be of *how soon* one could return to the free play of parties and of opinion. It was important that Roundheads and that American Revolutionaries thought that they upheld constitutional forms; but the claim became at certain stages very weak. What matters immensely was their subsequent conduct in power.

If, then, we accept (a) the pessimistic estimate of the contemporary social situation, and (b) the possibility of the speedy 'liberalization of Leninism'—which seems to be Malenkov's, and maybe Bulganin's and Khrushchev's, hope—then there really seems to be only a minor difference, *not* indeed between the optimistic view of constitutional socialism and the British Labour Party, on the one side, and the Communist Party, on the other, *but* between the pessimistic view of Laski and that of the Communist Party. It is a minor matter that he himself occasionally wrote against it in his early phases and later. On the whole, so far as there is a difference, there is some bias in favour of efficiency and clear-sightedness on the side of international Communism.

One can, of course, say that affability towards the rulers of Russia mattered a great deal, at the time of this debate, whereas the local Communist Parties, so frequently betrayed by high Russian policy, were and still are impotent mischief makers. But the watershed of opinion seems yet to lie, on this analysis, between the degreees of optimism or pessimism of our social philosophy and view of the social structure, and the consequent practical recommendations, including, as Laski said, "fighting side by side with the Soviet Union," should the issue arise. In my view this last dictum was the inevitable consequence of original judgements, doctrinaire and merely wrong.

That something *ought* to be done by the Free World to meet the Leninist or Bolshevik argument is, we have said, not in dispute. It is the theme of Mr. Paul Hoffman's informed book *Peace Can Be Won*. Here Mr. Hoffman, former administrator of the Marshall Aid Plan, with a rather peculiarly American sales emphasis in terminology but guided by patent sincerity, writes:

"The word [Propaganda] originally meant to propagate an idea or faith[1]. From the standpoint of this original meaning, it can be used to serve creative and moral as well as destructive and immoral ends. We must, I believe, start thinking of propaganda in these terms . . .

"In the area of seeking to influence and convince, the men of the Kremlin are immeasurably aided by something we have not yet crystallized to a sufficient extent: a body of doctrine, a product to sell. This body of doctrine originated in the studies of Marx and Engels, who envisioned a classless society in which the state 'withers away' and men live in peace and brotherhood. The fact

[1] *Cf*. The Society for the Propagation of Christian Knowledge.

that the theories of Marx and Engels, as they have been put into practice by Lenin and Stalin, have brought into being a dictatorship in which an élite group rules with brutality and ruthlessness has not prevented the use of the theoretical Marxist doctrine for propaganda purposes.

"To disseminate this doctrine, the men of the Kremlin have organised a vast apparatus . . . It is a major instrument of Kremlin policy and as such is directed by the potent Department of Agitation and Propaganda of the Communist Party. Both Lenin and Stalin gave meticulous attention to perfecting its program and techniques."

That anti-Bolshevik Resistance groups, for example in satellite countries, can be heartened by the clear re-enunciation of a propaganda, not unsupported by power, is the theme of Oleg Anisimov, in his book *The Ultimate Weapon:* and this at one time was the theme of Radio Free Europe, more cautiously of the Voice of America Radio, and indeed of Mr. Sumner Welles and of Mr. Foster Dulles. Containment would not be enough. The issue was one of morale. Stabilization and security could not decently be procured by diplomatic agreement among the Great Powers, more maleficent than any Holy Alliance, to enforce the perpetration of slavery of the smaller nations. This would be an odd consequence of two "Wars for Freedom". It is right to reach the conclusion of that eminent student of strategy, Captain Liddell Hart and his colleagues, in their study, *The Red Army* (1957), that the probability of Russian aggression varies directly with diplomatic Municheering and inversely with "the strength and will of freedom-loving nations", still with superior economic potential, "to resist". Here Mr. Walter Lippmann would seem to be quite wrong in his over-cautious or even timid judgements. The gamble must be seen to be so unlikely to pay that a 'war by miscalculation' becomes improbable. Those who deplored, on the contrary, 'moralism' and talk about 'principles', found with Professor Hans Morgenthau (German-born but now of Chicago), 'realism' to lie in attention Decatur-like to national power, although the influential Mr. George Kennan, who deplored a senatorial rhetoric of pulpit moralism, in his *American Diplomacy* did stress that 'principles' surely played an important role in national life and that nations, such as America, first had to practice these principles themselves.

Dr. Vannevar Bush, whom we have already quoted, in his *Modern Arms and Free Men*, writes:

"The power of ideas is great, given time, but the time may be long indeed when there is a force ready to exclude and distort them, backed by a secret police with tommy-guns . . . [Yet] here lies one of our opportunities. We certainly ought to be able to spread ideas, if we have them to spread. If the amount we spend on the competition between almost indistinguishable cigarettes, or between flavoured brands of alcohol known as whiskies, were used for the purpose, if the money spent on advertising cosmetics were diverted for the purpose, we could tell a very large number of people many things. They can be simple things but they are worth telling."

Indeed it is almost a *cliché* that some conquering power does, or could, lie in the ideas of liberty and the pursuit of happiness, democracy, law and social justice. We could add that, within the last few months, the Soviets themselves have become converted to the Common Law principle that 'no man is to be presumed guilty before trial' and have, through official Communist organs, condemned the court procedures of Andrei Vyshinsky, upon whom so many even in the West recently fawned. It is probably more solid to observe that, compared with military expenditure or economic aid, a coordinated campaign of propaganda of truth costs in money very little, however much it may cost in intelligence and devotion. (A happy display of these two last qualities is shown in Edward Steicher's inspired collection of photographs, *The Family of Man*.)

What, then, concretely, do we propose to do about it? Maybe our assumptions that it is all so easy may be marked by a *naiveté* which it is high time to discuss.

In the last forty years, and certainly not least in the last ten years, Marx-Leninism has advanced over a considerable portion of the globe—so widely indeed that (as Lenin noted) it has only to win India to pose as the official faith and philosophy of more than half the human race. This remarkable advance, almost unparallelled since the great days of Islam, has indeed been achieved with the Red Army in the background. Just as some modern historians, such as Professor Barraclough, hold that the advance, by sword and gospel, of Islam (later repelled in battles from Tours to Lepanto) marks the only real watershed between 'ancient' and 'modern' history, so maybe the advance of Marxism and the Red Army will be held to mark a like watershed, set by a political faith, in our own day.

Here at least Professors Barraclough and Toynbee would seem to agree that the decisive history of man is the history of his faiths. But any comparison with the Caliph Omar breaks down in so far as the conquest, for Communism, whether of China or of Czechoslovakia was not a military conquest by the Red Army.

Courage indeed is required, and this may be the message of Tours and Lepanto; but Mr. Adlai Stevenson is right when, in a recent speech, he insisted that future generations will regard it as ridiculous to suppose that issues of social economics or of ideas can be settled by shooting it out, any more than a watch can be repaired by behaving like an angry child and taking a hammer.

The conquests hitherto made by Bolshevik Communism, however backed by the Red Army in reserve, have been conquests primarily of a different order. Here lies its secret.

It advanced with a battle cry comparable to that of Islam—"God is One and Mohammed is His Prophet"; but even more, not less, than Islam it advanced with a gospel—a gospel not for soldiers with a sword, but for workers in the factories and even for peasants in the field.

It was a conquest by devoted disciples of the creed, the atheistic theology—by disciples and apostles such as Mao and Chou En-lai. It was a conquest where the hosts of Communism advanced like those of Joshua, encircled the opposition thrice, blowing upon the trumpets of propaganda. It was, at least in Eastern Europe—if not quite bloodlessly, and not without purges and genocide—a conquest where the walls of these places fell down flat, and the conquerors entered in to form the governments. Political systems are like fissionable material, which can be blown up by apt ideas. However, this is a game at which two can play. In the recent words of Marshal Bulganin, "Ours is a superior ideology." Here the West is confused and inert. We cannot long remain in competition against those who know their minds, if we do not.

In the light of this experience, the refusal of small-gauge, departmental-minded civil servants, moved by jealousy of other civil servants in Ministries of Information, to consider the problem of propaganda co-ordination can only cause a feeling of despair, and that those whom the gods will to destroy they first make mad.

The trouble, of course, is that this kind of problem carries the ordinary civil servant, politician or business man out of his depth. Even the trades union secretary can become a little canny about 'personal liberty' when certain trade union practices are discussed. 'In principle,' and with their lips, they may agree with the contemptuous dictum of that tough old practical politician, Georges Clemenceau. *Ce qui donne du courage, ce sont les idées* ... 'When you say "shut up!" they shut up... These revolutionaries of yours have about as many ideas as my boots. Envy and resentment—that's all they've got.'

But when the civil servant is asked by the old atheist Clemenceau, *le tigre*, to collect for himself, to support or to oppose, some fighting ideas, what should the poor fellow do—save obstruct? His *metier* is "to administer the act," not to provide original ideas to his masters. If only it were just a simple matter of traditional electioneering slogans! But the slogans fall flat. And the task is actually so difficult, and tends to touch the nerves of Western civilization on the quick.

It is noteworthy that it is not the civil servant or the politician or the capitalist business men but Catholicism, as with Father d'Arcy's *Communism and Christianity*, which has in many cases provided the intellectually respectable reply to Marx-Leninism—just as it has also, not least, provided the martyrs.

However the free world, which includes India and many Arab lands, can find formulae which, at least superficially, are not doctrinally or religiously limited. Particularly in areas of common values, such as the Anglo-Saxon world, Mr. Hugh Gaitskell can, on his visit to America, appropriately urge that we endeavour more "to speak with one voice." Before President Truman used the phrase, the then Foreign Minister of Australia and first father of the Colombo Plan, Sir Percy Spender, urged publicly (in words which he was so generous as to attribute to a memorandum by this writer) that "we struggle for the minds of men."

To this writer also President Eisenhower, then President of Columbia University and before he became President of the United States, declared that he was "fanatically interested" in this issue of the presentation of ideas, while deploring that "when the United States entered into the field of propaganda it took an awful panning," which must stop. It was President Eisenhower who, at San Francisco in August, 1956, added

57

that the issue is not only one of the mind but of a conviction that touches men's hearts and direct judgements of value. But still so little has been done. And much of what has been attempted, for reasons that are not clear but may connect with inadequately firm direction, has been abortive.

The famous remark, at his Cabinet meeting, of Lord Melbourne, placing his back to the door, "Gentlemen, I don't know whether this act is going to increase the price of corn or reduce it, but before we leave this room we will agree upon what we are all going to say," is scarcely relevant to an issue which touches the deepest recesses of the human spirit and has an almost religious bearing upon our interpretation of human civilization itself. Nevertheless, Lord Melbourne's remark did have a certain worldly wisdom, which the most Gallio-like, lethargic or sceptical politician might ponder, as touching the coordinated presentation of the Western case or indeed of the Free World case.

3

The stumbling block in this field is that, although we are all convinced that we stand for immensely important values for which rhetoricians would even be prepared to exhort men to die, we are exceedingly inarticulate, if not confused, about what these values and goals are. We are here discussing them, not in their quality as ultimate ethical ends of life, but because *we are still discussing the agreed political means of enduring peace, and we find Marx-Leninist world propaganda, and blue-prints, a grave obstacle to agreement on these means.*

The Marx-Leninist does not want a *détente* for peace except upon the basis of acceptance of these blue-prints, for which we as yet offer no alternatives that will, for example, convince the Indonesian. We think that we have a better basis for belief, that would issue in peace and even welfare— but we don't know quite what. We have to meet the criticism

58

that it might be better if we abandoned any political principles at all and, in dealing with the Soviets, "let the water find its own level." But we may suspect that, were the West to encourage 'indifferentism' and a cynical tolerance, while the Soviets continued to propagand Marx-Leninism, it is the Marx-Leninism that would win.

We could, of course, take Woodrow Wilson's Fourteen Points or, even better, we could take, as our foundation in what some call 'political ideology,' Roosevelt's and Churchill's Atlantic Charter—once this writer urged precisely such a course—and expand each clause, so as to make clear its implications and meaning, and we could say that we, in the Free World, stand for this. Or we might take the United Nations Charter of Human Rights and demand its implementation.

However, perhaps heeding Mr. George Kennan's exceptionally exacting advice that we should "show forth our light before all peoples" and attend first to our own examples, many people are more concerned with their *own* "pattern of life." There is "the American 'pattern of life' " and the British 'pattern of life.' And doubtless the French, and the Germans indeed and the Russians, have their own virtuous national patterns. This philosophy of 'national patterns' yet has one political weakness in common with fascism. It does not appeal to those who have not the privilege of belonging to that particular nation. And although, doubtless, these 'patterns' or folk *mores* or tribal ways are sometimes pleasant and ideal, whereas *fascismo* was not so pleasant, nevertheless there seems to be a certain agreed doubt, among the political philosophers of this Burke-and-claret philosophy, whether these 'idols of our market-place' can ever be exported.

They do not appeal with the magistral Jeffersonian fervour. They use the language of the upper-class club about what is 'done'. Unlike even the militarist Napoleon, their spiritual defenders do not carry, with their bayonettes, the standards that proclaim the Rights of Man, the sacred cause of humanity. The bones of these armies are not clothed in the vital flesh, the fervid and honorable, even if distorted, conviction about man, of the gospel of Lenin. They are poor little provincial growths, as if someone were to re-write the Bible by adding *Pickwick Papers*.

Maybe simple men will, without thought, die or live for their local village. But they will not die for, or live by, intellectual talk about 'patterns'. Indeed, with such a philosophy, how could we convince an Indian or an Indonesian that there was any common area to be called 'a Free World,' of which we talk so much, and in which he had partnership?

Patriotism itself, *la gloire de la patrie*, is of course another matter. Do we then inscribe Nationalism or National Sovereignty, as first principle, upon our banners? Interestingly enough, if not as first principle then as a principle, Molotov and even Stalin did come near to inscribing just this very thing. Maybe (and we shall discuss this later) it was one of the Soviet's few propaganda mistakes, even if so very nearly right. Stalin was the great Titoist, it seemed to say. Or should we rather lift up the standard of some new vision of man?

Hitherto we have assumed that there is some kind of what Walter Lippmann calls 'public philosophy' of the Free World; and indeed that this is approximately the Anglo-Saxon philosophy of Britain and, even more articulately, of America. From the lesser, more common-place 'American pattern of life'—which, if not of Hollywood, yet seems to emphasize, in recent Cinerama, the gambling dens of Las Vegas—or even from run-of-the-road patriotism (for American, but then also for Russian) we can perhaps afford to turn away to detect a more authentic philosophy of American genius. But here comes the rub. Where does that genius lead? And can we afford to follow it?

In the view of Professor Boorstin, of Chicago (but born

in the South), it leads to a new conservation of respect for local ways. The Indian will be invited to contemplate the Free World as displayed in Louisiana or Mississippi. In the rather maliciously perverse view of Professor Barraclough (successor at Chatham House to Professor Toynbee, and to whom I have already referred), North America probably does not belong to the European civilized world at all, but Russia, because it is Byzantine, does. We are indeed concerned with what Professor Barraclough calls 'a civilization's capacity for moral leadership', the kind of thing about which (especially when military leadership has gone) there is a great deal of loose talk. But are we to exclude America from this leadership?

Is the West in fact, as the Marxists and some also of the Free World allege, now culturally schizophrenic and spiritually bankrupt?

4

My answer is going to be 'no'. But I want to give reasons for that answer which can perhaps be heard without impatience even in the India which I know, and even in Indonesia. To do this, I have to discuss certain characteristic trends in contemporary North American philosophy, not without influence in Britain, which show far less fundamental distinction from Marx-Leninism than is generally supposed. We may either conclude that the supposed antagonism between American and Russian civilization is a matter of shadow boxing. Or we may conclude that the American philosophy of social goals has itself got on to the wrong lines. It is in urgent need of self-criticism to straighten itself out, if its synthesis is to offer what contemporary needs require.

It may be that it is not a case of America having failed the American 'intellectual' but perhaps, as Father R. L. Bruckberger, O.P., suggests, that, unassimilated or unassi-

61

milable, "perhaps the American intellectual has failed his country." By this is not here meant that he has failed to be just representative of his locality. To suggest, with Professor Boorstin, that the complaint is a mere querulous "Why aren't we more like Western Europe?" is to go off on a wrong scent. One is not so interested in the manners and customs of the native inhabitants of North America. The 64,000 dollar question is: Does the American intellectual rise to the level of moral and intellectual leadership in *human* civilization? Perhaps the downright statements in international affairs of President Eisenhower, since his 1956 Election—statements on the rule of law, the United Nations, freedom of political choice and human equality—have more, and not less, meat in them.

Nor is it to be supposed that contemporary Western European philosophy, in its academic statements, is in better plight to meet the needs of existence. Rather it tends to bow itself out with the excuse that what men think, as distinct from how and by what intellectual techniques, is not its concern.

The first objection to 'the American philosophy' of to-day can be stated in a paradoxical form. It is that this philosophy is at core Marxist and has, therefore, no spiritual weapons left with which to fight Marxism. Hence the embarrassment and hesitations. Although the objection may be false, it will bear examination. Although we may speak of a distinctive American philosophy or, perhaps better, 'climate of opinion,' admirably illustrated by the work of such philosophers as Pierce, James and Dewey in Professor Percy Miller's *American Thought*, there are several and diverse strains in that national thought.

The conventional Eighteenth Century orthodoxy of Washington, the deism of Emerson, the addiction to the French Enlightenment of Jefferson, deepening into the explicit rationalism and atheism of Paine, are all alike

62

elements in that climate. The national motto on the coins, "In God We Trust," appears to damn the notion of a secular state as have so many Presidential Inaugural speeches. And yet what conclusions a constitutional lawyer or Judge of the Supreme Court would be prepared to draw from this is another matter. The almost sacred constitutional doctrine of separation of church and state—which by a quaint irony, under anti-Catholic denominational pressure upon the Department of State in a clearly secular matter, prevents America, unlike India and Egypt, being represented in the Vatican State—is yet ambiguous doctrine. It may mean the repudiation of the establishment of an official church, as in England and Scotland; or it may mean that society so far as it is going to be organized through the state, and in its education, shall be exclusively secular, and no more Christian than Jewish or Moslem or Ingersollian atheist except by chance. Both themes have had their influence.

Nor is the second theme obliterated by the much higher stress in the United States than in Britain upon church attendance—60% as against 11%—as a condition of local approval. To educational secularism a powerful content is given in contemporary American thought by the influence of pragmatism, as a philosophy, upon the great American institutions for the training of teachers. The philosophy of 'Does it work?' and 'Will it succeed?' fits in admirably with the temper of mind which sees men as shaped by their external, material and economic conditions; which attends to 'ecology'; and which is immensely preoccupied with successful adaptation to conditions.

Senator McCarthy, amply endorsed, sprang from just such an insistence on local adaptation. The task of good living is regarded as a species of engineering problem. The interesting thing here is that the Russians do just the same. What I wish here to dissociate myself from is the American philosophy of such a representative popular writer as Professor

63

Max Otto, also (perhaps on the principle of point and counter-point) from Wisconsin, although born in Germany ; and to indicate the corrective importance of, for example, such a book as Camus' *L'Homme Revolté* or Colin Wilson's *The Outsider* or Merton's *Seven Storied Mountain*. The Marxists regard the issues all in the same secular and external or behaviorist way, as distinct from the true humanism which repudiates the assimilation of men to machines. No wonder that Maierkowski dedicated a poem to Chicago.

Secondly, Neo-Darwinism and Herbert Spencer had, at least in the last century, a vast influence upon American thought, so that, in *Lochner v. New York*, 1906, Mr. Justice Holmes had to protest that "the Fourteenth Amendment does not enact Mr. Herbert Spencer's Social Statics." Spencer himself substituted sociological science for any perennial philosophy in ethics; and not for nothing did Marx offer himself as 'the Darwin of the social sciences.'

In all these cases what had been the typical and traditional Western European humanist approach, something hitherto characteristic of 'Western European civilization,' was missing. Until a new philosophy of Humanism can be stated con-vincingly—by which I do not mean the half-forgotten philosophies of either Professor Irving Babbitt or of Professor F. C. S. Schiller but (let us say) the Christian Humanism of Erasmus—and stated in a fashion consonant with a yet older tradition of the human spirit, it is highly improbable that the philosophy of the Anglo-Saxon world (upon which I have commented in another book) will achieve any satis-factory synthesis. At least it is doubtful whether this philosophy, as especially expressed in America, with its denial of ethical absolutes and hyper-anthropological emphasis upon the relativity of ethics and 'naturalism,' will be able to make headway against that of Marx, however much both may call themselves 'democratic.'

Some, at least, of the clamour in the New World against

Marxism is merely hypocritical and is directed against other threats, for example to private wealth, than those which it pretends.

The objection, then, is that current Western philosophy is too unrestrained an ethical relativism, which ends in short-range success worship. In such a worship the greater social success is likely to win against small individual and pioneer attempts. If 'success' is the measure, Leviathan has it.

The third objection to characteristic American philosophy and pattern of opinion, as claimant to spiritual leadership in the Free World, can be put in another, but related, way. I would venture the further paradox that one real and fatal objection to Marx is that he was too much of a capitalist. And here again Americanism and Marxism are too similar.

Explicitly what I mean is that Marx indeed took the competitive economic theories of Ricardo and the Classical Economists, which Spencer with his neo-Darwinian exaltation of competition, developed, and which to-day Mr. Herbert Hoover still accepts, and stood them on their head.

Marx substituted, for the competition of business men which was supposed to be (in accord with some invisible workings of the natural law of economics) healthy for society, an equally or more fierce Darwinian competition of classes for survival, with the liquidation of the defeated. But, in developing this theme, Marx took over quite uncritically the psychology, not only competitive but aggressive, generally accepted in his time. This had been shaped by the French Hedonist philosophers, who derived, in their turn, their views from that venerable "atheist of Malmesbury", Thomas Hobbes.

That a better understanding of human nature would indicate, as alone sound, the disciplines of a psychology of cooperation, not of aggressive and neo-Darwinian competition, was a vision vouchsafed *neither* to Marx *nor* to the capitalist world of his day. The restatement of religion in psychological terms of the adventure of social trust may owe something to Jung but comes after Marx, and was as alien to his thinking as to that of Feuerbach. Men, in those days, worshipped a Darwinian devil.

Marx, as philosopher, suffers from certain fairly obvious logical defects which his devotees seek to cover up by fleeing, when pressed, from the theme that Marxist philosophy is alone right and better than all others, to the quite different thesis that the logic of his philosophy does not matter, except for idle bourgeois hair-splitters, because he was such a great revolutionary able to 'change' his followers by his inspired philosophy which, if not quite right, yet was good enough to uplift them.

We can say with such a Soviet writer as Leonov that "Bolshevism's treasury of ideas is something the Party guards as the apple of its eye." "The unshakable foundation of this possession is our Party's idea of the world, dialectical materialism." But, if so, it would be well to clear up such logical ambiguities as: (a) If the Dialectic of thesis and antithesis in struggle is fundamental to history, what happens to the Dialectic when the classless society is achieved; or is that socially harmonious society, which is the object of the revolution, itself broken up by further struggle (e.g. between skilled and unskilled, worker and bureaucrat) according to dialectic? (b) If everything is economically or materially determined at a given place and time, then the thought of Marx himself is so determined and, with change of conditions, *pro tanto* becomes obsolete thought.

That Marx's thought is dated is no serious charge against him. But it would help spiritual coexistence if Marxists would say so publicly. And we may add that what is peculiarly obsolete (and therefore obstructive to scientific progress) in Marx is his basic psychological suppositions. Human nature is, in quite essential matters, not as Marx portrayed it in the mid-Nineteenth Century—nor as Rousseau did either. Nor as did Ricardo (who never quite alleged that he talked of other than abstractions). Scientific advance can begin from here.

In America there yet still lingers the belief that mid-Nineteenth Century Capitalism, and its appropriate psychology, is a gospel to be proclaimed to the world by all solid men with a stake in their countries.

Patently, we have here first to understand what we mean by 'capitalism.' In one sense every economy in the world is based upon a certain conservation of capital, and this system is 'capitalism.' By 'private capitalism,' however, is traditionally meant something quite different, which historically connects with the psychological school of French Hedonism and anti-religious 'libertinism'; with the Nineteenth Century theme of enlightened self-interest in the acquisition of money; and with stress upon the profit motive as essential to a dynamic economy. (There are of course other and different Calvinist connections which Weber and Tawney have stressed, which are however also divergent from the rules of the Canon Law). Excessive stress on 'capitalism,' so conceived, means that national economy is to be judged in terms of private profits for those so situated as to be able to make them; and that the political order is to be adjusted to this system, which is to be treated as an ethical proposition, while any Christian inhibitions are to be relegated to Sundays.

I wish here to pass no criticism upon what, it is now suggested in America, should (scarcely felicitously) be described as 'competitive cooperative consumerism,' instead of 'capitalism.' However, as touching what the Classical Economists understood by 'capitalism,' at its best it has to be morally justified, as against the New Testament of blessing upon the meek and poor, on the basis of the Hebraic belief that increase of money and flocks are a sign of the approval of the Almighty, although presumably that approval is given rather to the industrious apprentice than to sharp business.

To the outsider the system can impress the critic as an unlovely exaltation of calculated selfishness, which can briefly be described as certainly un-Catholic—on which theme the researches of R. H. Tawney and Max Weber are relevant—if not indeed un-Christian.

I choose these words since the condemnation in the Social Encyclicals of Leo XIII and Pius XI are too readily forgotten as being directed *no less* against unbridled capitalism than against Marxist communism. The summary of the position by Pius XII, in 1946, can here be recalled:

"Only too often it happens that economic life and the employment of capital are no longer ruled by human needs in their natural and real importance. On the contrary, what needs are satisfied, and to what extent, is decided in the interests of capital and its profits. In consequence, it is not man's labour for the social welfare that attracts and uses capital, but capital which moves labour about like pawns in a game of chess . . . In the divinely willed order man would be master of most things by his labour; he would not be dominated by them."

Such statements, however, may be held to be irrelevant to a primarily Protestant and individualist America.

I am *not* here suggesting that either American or British 'capitalism' to-day is or could be a relentless exploitation of the economic situation for private profit, even for the widely distributed shareholders, or is incapable of being interpreted as a proper stress upon the economic independence, so far as practicable, of *all* individuals, competent to display creative initiative. An entire book could be written upon the theme, recently stressed by President Eisenhower, that, whereas European Continental capitalism has too often spelt the financial bolstering of a hereditary caste of industrialist families, into whose ranks the common worker cannot hope to penetrate, if not of absentee landlords (as once in Ireland), American capitalism is something quite other.

In a fluid social set-up a mobile organized labour can, and does, cooperate psychologically and economically in the development of an expanding economy, in which workers of ability can still expect to achieve managerial status. From the American point of view the stress upon this difference, if it can be exaggerated, is yet vital.

What I am saying is that there is too little ethical check upon irresponsible Western speakers who, without being cautious in their definitions of capitalism, identify America, not with a changing economy, but with a static capitalism of the almighty dollar; who seem to regard criticism of capitalism as criticism of a fundamental of the Constitution, which must be 'red' or 'communist' even if this criticism comes with the ancient voice of the See of Peter; and who quite fail to recognise that praise of capitalism as propaganda, in full half the world, is the kiss of death to American influence.

As the American press at least recognized, the attempt by an ex-President of the United States to identify constitutional non-Marxist Socialism with Leninist Communism plays directly into the hands of Bolshevik propaganda, even if Mr. Herbert Hoover, with his own belief in a classical economic individualism together with an *élite* of the Quaker 'inner light,' in his *American Individualism* and elsewhere, failed himself to see this. Even such an excellent foreign correspondent as Miss Marguerite Higgins occasionally falls into the same partisan *cliché* identifications and hence plays the Bolshevik game of identifying Socialism (and 'fuller' Democracy) with Bolshevik Communism.

Surely the more correct position is that the American economy, as recently emphasized by the President, and the British economy even as viewed to-day in Conservative quarters, is an economy of change, dynamic because experimental. Precisely in this it stands opposed to static economies *and* to static economic dogmas, as touching content, whether of Marx or of *laissez faire*.

C*

The empirical approach, granted that it is guided by a concept of social and of human justice, over against 'objectification' and the automation of man himself, is more vital, even when full allowance is made for the massive material success, although not unqualified, of Soviet experimentation. It will be pragmatic to learn in all quarters. The objection, then, on this third point, is that too much American philosophizing praises, along with local social assimilation, an aggressive economic competition founded upon a psychology also shared by Marx. This psychology is due to be superseded by a newer psychology which, for the gospel of mutual liquidation, the Darwinian devil taking the hindermost, substitutes the adventure of rational trust in those trustworthy.

There is a fourth objection to the now fashionable American position, to which I shall revert later. This at least is *not* a Russian position. The objection may be expressed as criticism of the belief, in some American quarters, that liberty and authority are absolutes and contradictories, not relatives and complementaries. The ultra-libertarian or democratic-nihilist position itself can be seen in the exaltation of opinion of any kind, as a kind of democratic sporting adventure in ideas which can afford to neglect mental discipline, since the standards of public education are themselves merely questionable opinions and must remain such.

The contemporary apostles or commentators on this point of view include Mr. Joseph Wood Krutch who, in *The Modern Temper*, rather melancholically reflects that man, far from having any *summum bonum* or unified end, is propelled forward explosively by his emotions to seek a thousand novel ends or values. Another is Mr. Archibald MacLeish who lays down, in a manner novel to the training of cultured men, that "the American Proposition is the proposition that if men are free to think for themselves and

70

to believe as they think" (apparently anything they think) "and to say as they believe—if men, *all* men, are free to make their own way by their *own* means to the truth which is *true for them, each one of them*—the world in which they live will be a better world . . . to think for ourselves, and say as we think, and do as we say" (italics mine).

Later indeed we are told very other things about 'labor in common of learning,' but here all the stress is upon variety as one of life's highest goods for variety's sake. This raises, indeed, the very profoundest of issues against Marxism. Sometimes indeed, in America, it is put forward as the core of the democratic case against Marxism—I believe by a misconception. It relates to marked subjectivism, atomistic individualism and contemporary existentialism. It makes ethics conditional to the individual, and to the time and place—conditional and relative. It gives indeed the flat answer to the very title of Mr. Lippmann's last book, *The Public Philosophy*.

There is, according to this view, no public philosophy in an American-type democracy. This so-called American Proposition passes over, from the progressivism of MacLeish, to Professor Boorstin's position, in his *American Political Genius*, that the American mind can oppose to Marxism no common view, no dressed battle front, but only customs local and obstinate, from Maine to Mississippi, which, relative to their locality, are as beyond challenge in up-state, rustic townships as any moral matter may be. It is a Humean bankruptcy of connected thought and the exaltation of antinomian provincialism. It can end as almost the opposite of what we here mean by rational humanism and culture. To this theme we must return later.

5

The labourer over much of the East neither has, nor expects to have, significant private property. Overpopulation

71

crowds the labour markets He comes nearer to the chance of himself sharing in ownership through a communal council or communist soviet than through a company dedicated to allegiance to 'the sacred rights of property,' but directed from abroad. When John Locke indeed spoke of these rights he was dishonest, since he did not produce a clear idea whether they appertained to all men or only to the possessors. The disadvantages, for the peasant promised land, of the Marx-Leninist 'blue print' only emerge later.

What, over against it, has to be emphasized is a concern, of integrity, for little people, not indeed only because they are little but because they are people, and because any system which begins by failing in respect for people as such, human beings, soon develops into a system injurious to the nerve of a high civilization. And it is in terms of its capacity for a high civilization that intellectually the human race is justified in existing, and is something more than a spawn of fungus and fauna, reaching to the pithecanthrapoid and recordable by science, upon this minor planet's surface.

National days of repentance and confession of sin may be good, if they are not hypocritical. No nation can find it easy to confess past sins and there are some political theorists of ingenuity, and even some heretical German theologians, who will hold that a nation collectively cannot sin. What we can expect is that, turning from the past, be it of slave-trading, imperialism or exploitation of labour, nations may attend to the more righteous vision of the future, while recalling their own prouder traditions.

Instead of harping on Capitalism or Socialism or like general names, we need to express ourselves in the Free World in words that have meaning for flesh and blood, corresponding to objective conduct which has fruit that can be judged. In the Soviet Union they are addicted to orgies of 'self-criticism', which they connect with authentic democracy.

In this chapter we have been endeavouring to clear the ground, before beginning constructive proposals, by a certain amount of needed 'self-criticism' of our Western fashionable ideas, including the one that we can, without compunction or further effort, claim for ourselves the title of 'the Free World'. The claim has to be earned and vindicated.

Moreover, advance will be made towards a genuine assessment of the situation, and towards an appeal which will carry conviction to a candid world, if we recognize that many of the offences with which we tax the Marxist, on better intellectual anaylsis we shall be seen to have maintained ourselves. They are, therefore, presumably not offences, so that here co-existence is quite possible. The differences, maybe, do not matter. Or, alternatively, (as I believe) they are indeed offences—such as ethical relativism, materialist behaviorism, pragmatic reduction of ethics to group success, an over-individualist pseudo-democracy or antinomianism than which Marxism could be better, too emphatic economic determinism, brave new world secularism, preoccupation with dominative power, treatment of human beings on an engineer's analogy with machines—but offences of which we have to confess that we have also been guilty, in our fashionable, easy thought, ourselves.

Until we rid ourselves of this schizophrenia and confusion at the centre of Western thought, it is improbable that, against those who link peace with acceptance of their own Soviet crusade of ideas, we shall present our convictions in a fashion that will either carry conviction in a hesitating world or will even display much faith in ourselves and our own integrity.

What the small nations of the world ask for, what the under-privileged ask for, is a new philosophy and psychology of cooperation, so that they may not only know but feel themselves to be wanted partners in a common human

73

cause. That philosophy and technique we need to offer. What, then, has the West to offer to the East, among what it believes in? The rough outline of this is our concern in the remaining chapters.

IV

WHO IS IMPERIALIST?

1

WHEN we speak of the political goal of the West or of 'the Defence of the West,' there is a preliminary and very real difficulty about what we mean by this 'West' and its civilization. Sometimes it primarily means North America; sometimes it includes Europe and North America; sometimes (as we have seen), for respectable historians, it means Europe only and includes Russia but excludes North America. Even so careful a writer as Mrs. Barbara Ward Jackson, in her *Policy for the West*, omits to begin by defining the term. Frequently it means Western Europe, ambiguously including Germany.

Anyway it does not mean China, whether National or Communist, or the Asian Soviet Republics. Its defence arouses no great emotional response in Oriental countries, but perhaps rather distrust. But it would be a misbegotten paradox indeed which identified 'the geographic East' with the Bolshevist bloc and 'the geographic West' alone with the non-Kremlin powers.

Sometimes, again, 'the West' is rather arrogantly identified with 'Christian civilization'—which authentically extends to Southern India and Ethiopia and is, in origin, Middle Eastern. A more useful phrase to discuss is, perhaps, 'the political goals of the Free World.' But what, we have already asked, does 'free' mean here? However, when we are discussing specifically 'political' goals, especially with reference to freedom, I shall make no apology for saying—and will expect most Asians to agree—that the political goals, not only of the United States, but also of the United Kingdom as a country, and even of the English as a nation will, on historical grounds alone, have to be considered. What are they?

In a recent, striking article Mr. Malcolm Muggeridge, of *Punch*, made the assertion—or his editor in the London *News Chronicle* did for him—that "the days of Great Britain are over." The argument is an easy one. Roberts of Kandahar and Kitchener of Khartoum are really dead. Under new conditions of aerial warfare Gibraltar and Hongkong are indefensible against serious attack. Malta and Singapore are in not much better condition. Clinging on to Cyprus is a rear-guard action. "Singapore is 'the pivot of our position in South-East Asia,' but we have no position in South-East Asia, and soon, very soon, will have none in the Middle East." If the rulers of Britain do not wish to be in the position of the Caliphs and the Great Moguls, with high pretentions and little power, then courageous politicians will have to be found to tell the British electorate that Britain is only 'a tight little island' once more.

With Mr. Muggeridge we are back with 'little Englandism' again. The Empires of China and of the House of Othman, the Empires of Romanov and Hohenzollern and Hapsburg have fallen in our own times. The turn of the British (and French) Empires is now coming. Only, it seems, the Shah and the immemorial Mikado will remain. The English must reflect that the Dutch and the Portuguese (who incidentally have quite a sizable empire as large as Europe) still contrive to enjoy themselves. We may add the Swedes and Danes. And the English must content themselves to be as they. The captains and the kings depart.

However, if we take up this argument, we must carry it further. Britain is *not* any longer a 'tight little island,' defended by its navy. The Channel, some say, thanks to air power has become a ditch. In the days of atomic warfare 'this blessed plot,' 'this little world,' has become supremely vulnerable as it never was in the days of Henry V and Elizabeth I, or of Chatham and Wellington. Economically it could never compete against a really united Europe, not to speak of a low-wage Japan. Comparison with Sweden is fundamentally unsound since Sweden is a country of small population (seven million) and large agriculture. Even agricultural France and Germany, which has always lived by its wits, are in better stead. Belgium perhaps alone offers a fair comparison.

What then are the British to do or aim at in this coming century when the great Leviathans of power all lie outside Europe—the United States, the Union of Soviet Socialist Republics, China? Vastly over-populated, with a high standard of living and a dangerously artificial economic structure which corresponds to her past, not her future, England still dreams (perhaps too timidly) of a 'new Elizabethan Age'; or of the warlike empire-building times of Chatham; or of the long-distant days of pioneering in the Industrial Revolution, when her industrialists and merchants, meeting little effective competition, with some degree of self-interest proclaimed the gospel of Free Trade and regarded not only Europe but the world as their 'economic oyster', to be opened for the asking by commerce and arms.

Artificially the great times of British capitalist prosperity, due to pioneering initiative, were prolonged, so that the real facts of the relative economic development of nations were concealed by all the prestige and advantages in trade of a massive 'going concern.' But now the illusion is over for those with eyes to see. Even the advantages in skill and experience of craftsmen, of shipping men, of bankers, are wasting. Only perhaps priority in insurance is left. Britain has "cooked her goose." England is up against it, although her protected business men, her workers, her electors, still do not recognize it. This is the story. Elgar's hymn will no longer be played.

Mr. Muggeridge concludes: "God who made us mighty, will make us weaker yet."

In Chapter Six I want to give the constructive answer to all this—to try to state the new political goals. Here I wish to comment on some of these factors which give substance to Mr. Muggeridge's lament and of which the development, breaking the crust of the old and bursting like lava into the new, seems to be inevitable. They are yet, in my view, not inevitable because of some iron determinism of history, but because Enceladus stirs and *ever increasing areas of mankind are accepting new ideas of how they would like to live which are incompatible with the old structure in politics.* As for Mr. Malcolm Muggeridge's conclusions, unless the English and Scots and the rest have lost all their old adaptability, I refuse to believe them.

2

It is idle to evade the reflection that the British people (like the French and Dutch) are saddled with association, in the minds of the rest of the world, with an Empire, beneficial indeed to some of its subjects (also like the French and the Dutch) but which masses of these subjects yet regard without favour, as an Empire like the rest and even an Empire slightly worse than some. That Shanghai was converted from a mudflat into a great city is something for which the Chinese ought to feel grateful—and would have perhaps felt grateful, had it only been a city of Chinese, built by Chinese for Chinese. But it was not.

The Hapsburg Empire, although it broke up thanks to the chance of defeat in war and owing to the heterogeneity of its peoples, was yet far more homogeneous than the British, deserved well in conducting the defence of Vienna against the Turk, and is still economically lamented by some of its peoples.

The British Parliament was politically far more liberal at

home than the Hapsburgs; but it was not always more liberal in India or in parts of Africa. The old Roman Empire made racial intermarriage one of the test rights of a Roman citizenship which became universal. It would have its parallel today if the Queen of England could be a Canadian who would, in all probability, be succeeded by an Indian, just as Spanish, Dalmatian and Arabian emperors held sway in Rome.

The English, however, were never prepared to accept their co-subjects as co-citizens in the same liberal fashion that characterized the political philosophy of Rome. They did not really believe that Cypriot and Kikuyu should enjoy the full *Magna Carta* rights of an Englishman, in the sense that the New England colonists had gone to war to insist that they must enjoy these 'rights of a free-born Englishman.' It was precisely the domination of one nation, as such, over another as such (which did not occur in late Rome) against which Rabindranath Tagore protested in his book *Nationalism*, Tagore himself being a humanist rather than any *enragé* nationalist.

For marching out of India, for reasons partly financial and military, but certainly also emphatically for reasons of political principles and ideas, swaying the home electorate, England has been rightly praised, not least in America—although the policy was, of course, stoutly opposed by Sir Winston Churchill who "had no desire to preside over the break-up of the British Empire."

Nevertheless in Africa and in such a small place as Cyprus the embarrassments of empire persist. Indeed the Cyprian[1] question, which is with us to-day, provides an apt illustration. Here also it may be prophesied with some confidence, at this time of writing, that the recent policy of Sir Anthony Eden, who "embarked with such loud reason to the Cyprus

[1] My Greek friends tell me that this is the correct use and 'Cypriot' a word of more ambiguous meaning.

79

wars," will be reversed by his successors, if not by himself. It is to the great credit of the British political genius that this is likely to be so. The reader who is concerned with the background of this policy may well read the work of the English sometime editor of a local Cyprus journal, Mr. Percy Arnold, in his *Cyprus Challenge*. Let us consider Cyprus for a moment.

In law, of course, the people of Cyprus are liege subjects of the Queen of the United Kingdom, and to use arms or to conspire against Her Majesty's Governors, who have final power of life and death—not indeed beyond appeal but, oddly, beyond obligation to stay capital punishment before the appeal is heard in London—is to embark on treason.

This legal position must, however, be taken in the moral and political context of the fact that the said sovereignty over the allegiance of thousands of souls and 'free men' was bought by Benjamin Disraeli from the Sultan of Turkey for a cash payment of the excess revenue and a promise to safeguard the rest of his dominions against Russian encroachment, rather as the Princes of Hesse used to buy and sell their subjects for cash. The sentiment of allegiance is, therefore, to say the least precarious.

The great Liberal statesman, William Ewart Gladstone, when denouncing what he regarded as the inexpungeable tendency to villainy of Disraeli and "the insane covenant," expressed the hope that Cyprus would soon be united to its Greek homeland. There was, of course, no question of Cyprus historically 'belonging' to the Greek State, since the Greeks themselves for millennia had not belonged to any such state (or the Italians to Italy) for the excellent reason that it did not exist. The Aphrodite of Paphos yet laughs in the face of the Colonial Office officials who suggest that Cyprus is not culturally as Greek as Greece herself, laughs in the face of Britannia with the arm of an 'unspeakable Turk' (now become 'honest John Turk') round her waist.

Two factors, however, complicate this picture, the one (as Disraeli foresaw) imperial, and the other of nationalism itself. These factors apart, it must be confessed that the British propaganda case was, and is, singularly weak, and of a kind which (rightly) usually makes Americans, to put it mildly, very unhappy. It has chiefly consisted in suggesting that the Cyprians would be far worse off in pocket if they succumbed to nationalist patriotism. Sometimes it has looked as if the British, who had lost the power to stand up to big peoples, were compensating themselves by pushing around the small folk.

The first reservation to this ready censure is that the moral and democratic right of self-determination must yield to necessities of empire which affect the lives of far larger numbers of people than those in Cyprus. Even the League of Nations in its early days had to admit that the Wilsonian principle of determination was conditioned by some limit in the smallness of numbers of those seeking self-determination—in the case of Cyprus rather over a quarter of a million—and also in the strategic importance of the area in its effect upon the pursuit of happiness of much greater numbers. For example, rightly or wrongly the Soviet Union is not prepared, in Karelia, to let a foreign frontier come too close to Leningrad.

At the beginning of the century there was 'a route to India,' and indeed to Australia, which was regarded as a prime object of imperial defence. It involved Gibraltar, Malta, the Suez Canal (although here there was, very foolishly, only a lease) and Aden. At this moment its strategy raises awkward problems for the autonomous statehood of a still pro-British Ceylon. It may be said that this 'all British route' to-day is "a route to nowhere"; but in fact it has changed, but not decreased, its importance as being a route to the sources of oil supply. The loss of the Palestinian Mandate and of the Suez Canal, both of ambiguous sovereignty, has made Cyprus as an air base (or as *containing* air bases) of high importance. It can be said that this consideration must take precedence of the sentiments of Greece, a country for patriotic and historical reasons hitherto perhaps the most friendly to Britain of any on the European Continent.

It can indeed also be said that such a Cyprus base is important for NATO defences; that the present situation devastates the friendly relations of NATO Powers; that the British Conservative Government's attachment to NATO seems to be of a character less than ardent; and that it is NATO, not Britain, that should make the arrangements for bases in Cyprus. This theme ignores, however, the imperial trail of oil (like the older trails of gold and steel) which is of key importance, not to NATO, but to Great Britain itself. It may be answered that NATO (supposing the British are loyal in support of it) has the strongest possible interest in seeing that the British Navy and airforce gets oil. But perhaps this guarantee is not enough.

How far, then, has a country a right to subordinate, through empire, the political preferences 'for freedom' of a smaller number of people to its own vital metropolitan needs? Maybe we feel that it is merely just too bad that the British, sitting on top of one of the biggest single blocks of fuel in the world, should yet recklessly have placed themselves in a position of dependence upon a fuel which springs up in ancient Arab lands. This, however, ignores a technological change: whatever happens to the navy, an air force can't be run on steam. It is no complete reply to say that, as a matter of morals, Britain should never have put herself, in the first place, into an artificial and unnatural position of economic dependence; or that not only Britain but every other country in the world would doubtless be most happy, if allowed, to have an empire (with power over other peoples) which, until the arrival of peaceful atomic power, would in their national interest and security give them oil. Perhaps only a better United Nations can co-ordinate, with justice, these conflicting claims. There is a second reservation to be made, not to recognition of the obsolescent character of imperialism, but to too facile censure.

The imperial factor in Cyprus (which I have chosen as an apt and typical illustration of the wider issues involved) is re-enforced by a national factor which complicates the principle of self-determination. In various parts of British Africa (as in the Southern United States) there are white minorities or near-minorities which hold political power in disregard of the preferences of the Negro inhabitants. According to Marx-Leninist theory these oligarchic minorities should be liquidated—unless indeed they 'join the Party' and remain as commissars . . . But what are we to say where it is a majority which, in the event of majority self-determination, is thought to be likely to oppress the minority—for example, the Greek Cypriots, with 90% of the population, to oppress the Turks with 10%? Shall there be further self-determination of the minority, and is this geographically possible?

Not only the strategic and imperial claims of Turkey are involved—as was said in the far-gone days of Venetian rule, "the importancy of Cyprus to the Turk"—but also the democratic rights of the Turkish natives in Cyprus. We may speak of the habits of "the unspeakable Turk" in the days before Mustapha Kemal made him an honest man. We may say that even modern Turkey is but a thinly veneered dictatorship, whose views have little claim before the world's democracy and that even the greatest of Turks, Ataturk, was no democrat as we and most Greeks understand the word; and that the British are thrusting Hellas, with all its potential submarine bases, into Soviet arms while talking, to alarm the Americans, about Hellas "perhaps going Communist."

83

We may deplore the stirring up of the cinders of ancient Greco-Turkish enmities which it was one of the finest achievements of the League of Nations to allay; the excessive British use of Turco-Cyprian police; the failure to develop the mood which led the loyal Turkish *mufti* in Cyprus to express belief in the desire of all Cyprians to live together in amity.

It may be said that the British Government, which under Mr. Leo Amery regretted that "Gandhi did not speak out against violence," to-day is bone-headedly repeating the same regrettable follies—follies, once committed, so difficult to undo. The problem of the effective guarantee of minority rights yet remains; and imperial power may seek, and even find, some justification in terms of it.

The withdrawal of imperial power from India issued, it will be recalled, in the partition of that sub-continent. The good and the evil are not so clearly separable as might be hoped. The case of Imperialism, then, as so often in history, can be urged to be not entirely simple. Nevertheless, moral judgements on goals, not disconnected from political judgements on means, have to be made. If we shirk the issue, then, in propaganda, the Soviet blue-print for world peace, thanks to world conquest by their ideas, will prevail.

3

Closely related to the problem of Imperialism is that of Colonialism. It is yet useful to separate and distinguish the two. Australia and New Zealand clearly began as British colonies. The British *raj* in India was an Empire. Although there were many administrators, the number of English tea-planters and the like in India were never enough to constitute a *colonia*.

Similarly Goa is rather a sphere of Portuguese imperialism than a Portuguese colony, populated extensively by people of pure Portuguese blood, in the sense that France has tended to colonize Algeria. The Gold Coast has for long been described as a British Crown Colony, but it was indeed rather a part of the British administrative empire. On the other hand, the white inhabitants of the Highlands of Kenya are precisely British colonists.

That there are political objections to a Colonialism under central administrative control the whole story of the independence of the United States demonstrates. The development of the Dominions and Commonwealth is a vast plan or policy to obviate these difficulties. But these objections to a Colonialism which has not yet reached the Commonwealth confederation stage are of a different order to the objections to Imperialism, as that domination of one nation over another of quite different culture which Tagore discussed.

Or, to change our terms, Emigrant Colonialism can be a very different thing from Imperial Colonialism. As is sometimes said, the objection to much Colonialism is that, lacking massive homogeneous immigration and rejecting a 'melting pot,' it is 'not colonial enough.' (In America it is the melting pot itself which has melted.) Even as touching Imperial Colonialism, before we denounce it without reservation, a prudent man will do well to pause and recall certain interim considerations. Under present circumstances, self-determination in South Africa, in the Rhodesias, in Central Africa, has every likelihood of meaning the determination of the white minority to govern (at least to a preponderant degree, if not exclusively) the Negro majority.

It is a significant thing that a Commissioner of London City Police, who went out to the chief police post in Kenya, has never denied that the reason for his resignation from the Kenya post was that he was made to understand that to prosecute for legal offences certain white settlers would be politically inexpedient. Later he has been unfairly called, by the Minister without Portfolio of Kenya, 'an indiscreet policeman.'

It will be recalled that when M. K. Gandhi was assaulted in South Africa, on a colour-bar issue, it was no local magistrate who took action. It was no other than Joseph Chamberlain, then Colonial Secretary, who cabled that Gandhi's assailants were to be arrested forthwith and put on trial. It emerges, therefore, that there are certain circumstances where a strong Colonialism, by which I mean a firm and almost ruthless Whitehall control over settlers who, while escaping home taxes, ask for imperial armed support, may be in the best interests of the majority of the inhabitants and of the prestige of the whole Empire.

4

The history of the Soviet Union is one both of traditional Russian Imperialism, especially Great Russian, continuing since the days when Peter the Great confronted the short-lived Swedish empire, and also of Colonialism. The story indeed of Russian expansion, across the slightly populated plains of Siberia, to the Pacific Coast, and indeed to Alaska, is too little known to people familiar enough with the British, French and Spanish stories. This empire ends, as is easily forgotten, in a common frontier with the United States.

In part the tale is one of authentic emigrant colonization, only differentiated from that of New England, Quebec and Australia by travel across land, not sea. Hence it becomes rather assimilated to that migration of the covered wagons travelling across the North American continental mass. In relation, however, to the Moslem Turcoman inhabitants of Southern Siberia, to Bokhara and Samarkand, and to the frontiers of India, Afghanistan and China, it is one of imperialist expansion, as was recognized in the days of the Crimean and Afghan Wars. It was no other than Marx who commented upon this Russian imperialist expansionism and stated, from his studies, that the Russians have to be stood up to, "in which event they retire decently enough."

86

Over against this imperialism, deeply set in the Russian tradition but to-day assuming more indirect methods, has to be set the nationality policy of Stalin, which was perhaps that dictator's most successful enterprise in policy and which is one of the few of his policies being renewed to-day. However, the story of the purges in the Ukraine and of the transportations, verging on genocide, of whole peoples such as the Don Cossacks and the Volga populations of German stock, about which Stalin made no bones in speaking to Sir Winston Churchill, indicate the very sharp limits to this departure from imperialist centralization.

The Western world has, therefore, insisted that Soviet Communism is not simply an ideological campaign of emancipation. This is surely a key-point of Western propaganda. As much as Napoleon's interpretation of the French Revolution, it is imperialistic—and more persistently so than was ever practicable for Napoleon's brief empire. The argument, moreover, that the great imperialisms, that spell for others absorption, have been those of the outstanding land Powers, and that the maritime Powers have traditionally been the supporters of national independence, has in fact carried weight.

It can be suggested that, in the Far East and in South Eastern Asia, no single factor weighs more heavily against the expansion of Kremlin authority than the fear of Russian interference with that newly-won national independence, with its proud banners that awake the fanatical loyalty of these peoples who have newly achieved statehood. That this was the core conviction and prime belief of the Indonesian Republic, the world's fifth largest state, was made very clear during his goodwill visit to Washington of President Sukarno. President Sukarno, in Italy, has re-emphasized (as I have endeavoured to do in this booklet) the outstanding importance of the campaign of ideas, and of the emotions aroused on behalf of the idea of national freedom.

However, although the Americans, with a good record in the Philippines and recently in Puerto Rico, can here go scot-free on the political and administrative level (I do not discuss the financial), every act of imperialism—by which I here mean the over-riding of the political wishes of one people for the advantage of those of another nation—on the part of Great Britain or France destroys the propaganda force of the Western argument for freedom.

5

Her Majesty's Opposition in Britain has consistently opposed the policy of the British Administration as touching Cyprus obtaining in the early months of 1956, not least on the ground that the banishment of the Ethnarch, Archbishop Makarios, elected representative of the Greek population (as his predecessors were under the Sultans), could only lead, as Earl Attlee has said, to a deterioration of the situation, reminiscent of the Irish 'troubles.'

Along with this have gone negotiations offering too little, and that little too late, with the execution of 'teen age boys and with mutual terrorism between those who stood by their right in law and those who stood by their moral right in patriotism. In fairness it should be added that, in a slightly different context, in May, 1956, Sir Anthony Eden said that "the world will have the right to call itself civilized when racial arrogance is universally condemned both by instinct and by conviction."

It would be well if the West, aspiring to the leadership of the Free World, could put on its banners a condemnation of Imperialism, as here described, and of that kind of Colonialism which we have called 'imperial colonialism'. Since there have been heated protests in British governmental circles against either of these labels being applied to their policy, on the ground that it was inspired by ignorance or malice, such a clear repudiation should not present undue difficulties. This,

88

of course, does not mean that such imperialism, like Mercantilism or *laissez-faire*, has never represented a stage in progress or a lesser evil. We need to be cautious in dealing in dogmatic abstractions. The condemnation is a declaration of future policy. It might be well if Britain should do this, as it turns its Empire into a Commonwealth. *But is this possible ? Is it policy or rhetoric ?*

As one contemplates the million and a quarter French colonists in Algeria (some of whose fathers and even grand-fathers were born there), the white settlers, Dutch and British, in South Africa where the relation to the Negro is essentially imperial and based upon control of arms, the statement of the connection between the strategic control of Cyprus, Arabian oil and British industry—in Sir Anthony's Eden's words, an issue "as simple as that"—doubts will arise in the minds of every practical man. Would it not be wiser to 'do a deal,' to pardon the brutal transgressions of Stalin, in order that Russia's strong men may look the other way about our smaller, but less well rationalized, trespasses?

This argument rests on the assumption that there is no other way out. If Britain, recently the world's greatest capitalist, imperialist and colonialist Power, although now outdistanced in imperialism by Russia, says 'An End to Imperialism,' then Britain starves . . . But is this true? And is there no other way? Sir Anthony says that Britain "must be either a Great Power or nothing." Mr. Malcolm Mugger-idge, a high Tory, replies that "this is nonsense," that Sir Anthony is talking bosh in the language of conventional *cliché*. Clearly there is a case here to be investigated—and one fraught, if the wrong decision is taken, with immense perils.

The British, unlike the Romans, have always been muddle-headed in their notions of empire. In the later days of Rome, as we have said, every freeman of every race alike could regard himself as equally a Roman citizen. Whatever this meant in politics, in law it meant much. But, although a Scotsman, a Welshman, and even an inhabitant of the lesser British Isle, could regard himself as British, in fact they have not regarded a Cyprian, a Singalese or a Kaffir as British. Yet in law all these were British subjects and most were "nationals of the United Kingdom and Overseas Possessions." The words 'subjects' and 'possessions' themselves indicated an archaic mind.

The Hapsburg Empire indeed was archaic enough, but at least its members, in European terms, shared common values and a common culture—although they did not share enough. The British Empire is the biggest political agglomeration of 'coloured men' in the world and has scarcely made any pretence of common culture or values, save as imposed. This is its weakness. It has indeed grown up, from arms and trade, "in a fit of absent-mindedness" such that the Briton does not himself know what just the word 'British,' which includes Welshman and Zulu, means. It is to be hoped that 'the Commonwealth,' from which Mr. Nehru has excluded the word 'British,' will do better. The older Commonwealth, which was strictly Colonial, is at least a reasonably clear concept.

What then of the economic and practical situation? It may be that the French colonists, unless they want to fight a war of extermination against Islam, will actually do better with an independent but allied Algeria. In the wider British field the situation is more hopeful than for the French. For Britain to say, "we must have oil or we shall starve, and to have oil we must have Bahrein and Kuwait and Cyprus, and maybe Palestine or the lion's share of the Suez Canal," invites the reply: "You had coal in abundance when others had not. Why should you claim by force to have oil which others desire? Invite in Italians as your miners." The motto "what Curzon held let Curzon hold" provides no adequate answer.

Equally it could be said, with a Conservative Minister of the Crown, it's "not enough only to produce." This can only add to difficulties, unless we can also sell in the markets of Europe and the world. We starve unless we win these competitive markets. But shall we add, with the mercantilists, "therefore we must conquer large areas in order that we may have consumer markets protected for our goods?" If we have unfortunately based our economy and strategy upon a lease in the Suez (in very typical Nineteenth Century finance-capital style) which lease soon ends, are we to demand a new deal without consent merely because some petty army chief may, in Levantine fashion, have 'jumped the gun'? Do we not do better to identify our claims with that of all other trading nations which look to see the establishment of a High Authority by consent, preferably, for Fuel and Transport, including Arab consent?

Admittedly the position of Britain is highly artificial. Her past fortune, and the assumption of its continuance as being in the unchanging nature of things, could be the present misfortune. It is not a matter of oil only, but of the whole economy. In the words of Mr. A. W. Tuke, Chairman of Barclay's Bank, one of the four great Joint Stock Banks of Britain:

"Economic necessity and political ambitions are pulling in opposite directions . . . Economic prosperity seems to demand a union which is repugnant to the political or national prejudices of the peoples concerned . . . unless some solution such as I have described is found within the next few years, economic factors, in fact the threat of starvation, will eventually compel the various nations to give up these national prejudices."

This brutal but just comment indicates the route out. Sir Anthony Eden may indeed be right that the modernizing of the British economy, which will mean a shake-up which many will bitterly resent, is "more important than foreign policy". But even modernization of production alone will not solve (since others can modernize too) the problem of markets.

As touching Cyprus the answer may well be, as has been apparent from the first, that the British Government should announce a date, as the Americans did in the Philippines, beyond the present but perhaps declining 'cold war', when a plebiscite will be taken, by the results of which the Imperial Government will abide, without a craven knuckling-under to (of all people) such dubious democrats as the Turks—with a precedent constituent committee to draft a fundamental act embodying adequate guarantees of minority rights.

Cyprus is, however, only an illustration. The issue is one of basic principle. I assume that the natives of the United Kingdom or the British Islanders would not be prepared to see every subject of the Empire have, like the Maltese, a vote in the Imperial Parliament in Westminster.

This logical solution discarded as undesirable, *the other path must then be firmly trod.* The route of continued imperialism by military or economic domination must be seen as a false trail, even for the lasting solution of domestic problems, including inadequate fuel production in a country built on fuel.

The route of freedom and of leadership is to declare categorically against Imperialism, and hence in favour of *a Commonwealth of British Nations extending into a wider Community, and into a Commonwealth of the Free Nations of the World, and in favour of the integration of the present nations,* with their Seventeenth Century state boundaries, into wider economic, social and even political units, within the context of one world. It is also to be seen in a readiness to appeal to wider international integrations (not yet global), such as that of the United Nations and NATO, as to a Common Market, for a route out of the impasse of Cypriot and Egyptian disputes. This building, not only of one world, but on closer regional integrated units of friends, was indeed what the liberal genius of the Republican candidate in America of 1940, Wendell Willkie, was led to advocate. *But we have still to ask ourselves, as we raise this banner, "What of Africa and its races?" and "What are the appropriate homogeneous units with whom we shall be content to risk our lives and national fortune?"*

V

BORN EQUAL

1

THE Soviet propaganda to the youth of the world is that the Soviets lead a crusade of emancipation. To desert this crusade is said to be the road, not of peace, but of imperialism. It is a propaganda of immense appeal. On this basis one of the world's sourest tyrannies has been built up, under Stalin (about whom the rulers of Russia to-day, as well as Trotsky yesterday are witnesses), but also under Lenin, whose fanaticism was so uncompromisingly described by Winston Churchill.

In the past men have asked for liberation from this tyranny, and to-day throughout much of Eastern Europe, despite what some experts with cold feet may have said in conflict with the heroism and dignity of which man shows himself capable, they ask for its relaxation. But the temper of Western democracy, which was indicated well enough in the British elections of 1945, makes clear that liberation must not apparently, at least for the present, be by preventive war, such as perhaps should have occurred in 1936, "the big stick" or equivalent police action. Nor is democracy even adapted to the long, depressing pressures of economic 'cold war', which the rulers of Russia have been able to wage by ruthless reduction of consumer goods for the workers.

It follows that, as the non-Communist and Communist peoples of the world increasingly meet and mix, what will be decisive, in the great debate, is which set of ideas have most appeal to the newer electors, the students, the world's youth.

The police state and centralized imperialism of Russia, the horrid succession of police chiefs ending in Beria, 'the British imperialist spy,' whose minions now perish in the plutonium slave camps of arctic Northern Russia—all this is no advertisement for Marx-Leninism and will make few converts. The expansive imperialism of the Soviet Union is liable, as I have said, to be regarded with alarm by peoples proud of their new independence. But industrial resentment, even in State-owned factories and mines in Europe, is always likely to look to the extreme 'Parties of Action.' The under-privileged, bitterly poor population of Asia, as of Africa, are likely to feel almost any change to be one for the better. Paradoxically, there will be fascist-minded persons who feel that, in the economic strains of the next decades, only the dictatorial ruthlessness and 'red fascism' of the Communist Party can discipline, with the abolition of free trade unions, the working masses in their lower echelons. As an Oxford teacher, Mr. John Plamenatz, has remarked : "Bolshevism has appealed more strongly to intellectuals than to workers in the West. Perhaps they like the energy with which it drives the 'inarticulate' and 'stupid' masses to work for the 'ultimate good of society'." One recalls Edmund Burke's cat-like metaphysicians. There is always a spiritual kinship between the black and the red fascism.

Against this the slow appeal, to reason and discussion and tolerance, of democracy, whether parliamentary or also (as I hold) 'pure' and plebiscitary, strives to win men's minds. But it is hampered when mud can be thrown, a mud that sticks, against French and British 'imperialism.' No less it is hampered by the charge brought of 'fascist racialism' against the Southern United States, and against some British Dominions. They are not charges which can be laughed off or dismissed as mere mis-representation.

The instinctive response of most Americans, especially from the North, would be to point out their equal protection under law is "the law of the land" or to recite the words of the Declaration of Independence, drafted by that great Virginian, Thomas Jefferson. "We hold these truths to be self-evident, that all men are created equal, that they are endowed by their Creator with certain inalienable Rights, that among them are Life, Liberty, and the Pursuit of Happiness." America has a clear record on 'Colonialism.' It patently dislikes even having to support its friends where this charge can be made. Is she equally vindicated, or not, as a challenger of racialism and of all forms of human inequality?

No human affairs are perfect, but there is a fine American record of racial integration, on orders over-riding peremptorily all prejudice, in the armed services; of appointments of Negro police in the great cities; of Negro magistrates sitting in courts; of the offer of an Assistant Secretaryship of State to such a man as Dr. Ralph Bunche. There is the magnificent and unanimous recent record of the Supreme Court. The Soviet record of the disregarding of any colour bar, in an equal servitude of Asians and Europeans under the yoke of Kremlin orders, seems unimpressive by comparison, however it may appeal in areas which smart under the galling recollection of British traders who assimilated, under one veto, dogs and Chinese.

Alack! this is not the whole of the story. In one British Commonwealth country—the Union of South Africa—one sees a patent attempt to set up a racial boss-dom. Who shall blame the African for turning for his hope to the mischief-makers, behind whom stands one of the greatest military Powers on earth, just as in the beginning of the last century the Central European turned for hope to the tyrant Napoleon, who yet offered the Civil Code? And so, too, in the Southern United States, not only is justice, as between white and black, clearly perverted on occasion (not without fine records by white lawyers at great risk) but recently there has been developed the doctrine of 'Interposition' of State authority, in defiance of the authority and unanimous judgement of the Supreme Court. Mr. James Byrnes, Governor of South Carolina, has indeed frankly written that "the Supreme Court must be curbed." The appeal is to some local *mores* of discrimination, some picayune and provincial 'pattern of life.'

2

The issue of Racialism is the great issue of our day. As the world grows smaller and populations more mobile, it becomes acute as never before. Perhaps the most powerful single element in Communist appeal, in a world of which the vast majority of the population is 'coloured' but where power still lies or has until recently lain with the natives of the European peninsula, is just here. Here civilization especially has to vindicate itself; but here emotions are most roused.

Oddly enough this strength of feeling about 'colour,' India apart, is apparently recent. It is the sentiment of Tooting Bec and of Memphis—not of course the ancient Memphis, the cradle of human civilization, which was a coloured man's city, but Memphis, Tennessee. If Moses was a Semite, Pharoah was, of course, a coloured man. In ancient Hellas the sentiment of 'difference' took a rather different form, as a feeling of immeasurable superiority to 'the barbarians,' to Persians and even more to the barbarous ancestors of almost all modern Europeans, including the 'stupid' Britons. But Racialism is not noticeable in Rome or in the Middle Ages, when the slaves were so frequently white European prisoners of the Arabs.

The Aga Khan points out that racial feeling was not general among the earlier English traders in India, but came in as a matter of snobbery with the wives of the middling employees, brought out on steam-boats from London *suburbia*. It is not marked in the older civilizations of Spain, Portugal or even France. Apart from the Indian Brahmin with his caste, it is especially a Nordic phenomenon, where skin contrasts between almost-albino and almost blue-black become maximal. From the point of view of the Chinese, who regards himself as normal, the self-styled 'whites' appear to be 'hairy red barbarians,' rather like monkeys.

The matter cannot, however, be argued only at this level. The challenging statement of principle is that human beings are 'born equal.' Is this true or is it what Bentham called 'bawling on paper'?

The answer must, I think, be that human beings are not equal and are not born equal. And it is difficult to build a science of political truth upon the basis of a false statement.

Jefferson indeed, in the original draft of the Declaration, had also stated that men were 'born independent,' until some member of the Continental Congress, having the common sense to recall his own total dependence as an infant upon his mother, had this phrase stricken out. In an interesting passage Lincoln stated that it had been no part of the intention of the signatories of the Declaration of Independence to suggest that all men were equal in all respects; but this common sense qualification removes much of the drive from the principle. Indeed one may suspect that Jefferson, as a Welshman, had every intention to gather behind the banner of Equality all the intensity of feeling—and of pent resentment—which egalitarianism can engender.

Recent philosophers, such as Professor T. V. Smith, have shrewdly pointed out that much of the emotional force which gathers behind this doctrine of *Egalité* is really not so much concerned to affirm equality—"all are equal, but some are more equal than others": "the workers are equal to the bourgeois and indeed a damn sight better." Rather it is concerned, as Professor R. H. Tawney insisted in his book *Equality*, to repudiate artificial, functionless and unjust inequalities, economic inequalities, insolent and glaring in world history, which affect the nutrition and very stature and expectation of life of children due to poverty, or inequalities due to wealth gained by speculation or to power gained by those methods which Pope Gregory VII compared to those of Cain and Romulus, the fratricides.

Human beings in truth are not equal. They are not equal in physique or strength. They are not equal in intelligence or gifts. It is a matter of the chances of life and of heredity, not of race, nation or class. They are not equal in ability. They are not equal in moral character. The demand for equality of opportunity rests logically upon the assumption that young men of superior ability shall not be prevented by lack of wealth or privilege or by class prejudice from demonstrating to the world that individual inequality of ability and that superiority to their fellows. If all men were actually equal, or born such, there would be no point whatsoever in equality of opportunity, since opportunity would display nothing that was not already universal, a monotone of gifts.

In fact human beings' humour and common sense, whatever a Caliban envy may say, makes them quite well aware that men are by no means equal; and that progress depends upon the unusual ability or ex-cellence of the extra-ordinary and of the few, as well as upon the concurrence, upon the gift for accepting good leadership, and upon the good-will of the many. The trouble lies with the false, bogus and 'pseudo' inequalities. What Aristotle said that the many were likely to have, as much as the few, was the quality of judgement. Upon the ordinary man's possesion of this quality rests the philosophy of the Anglo-Saxon jury system, to which Mr. Justice Humphreys has recently paid, as touching its practical success, such high tribute. Nor does Hobbes' tricky Iago-like argument, about no one knowing who may be superior in quickness on the draw with a stiletto on a quiet night, really upset the argument about diversity of gifts. Lenin had no illusions about human equality, nor Marx, in his *Critique of the Gotha Programme*, either.

True although this denial may be, there has been extreme reluctance on the part of most human beings in recent times, a sense of shame or of betrayal, in admitting this. In part this may have been a matter of wishful thinking or of jealousy of the commonplace against the excellent or even of that conspiracy of the second-class against the first-class genius of which John Stuart Mill, the father of modern Liberalism, complains so bitterly in a classic passage.

But there is yet more to it than this. There is an undefined sense of 'being undemocratic' and indeed of compromising with evil. Those most keen to emphasize man's inequality seldom proceed with the logic to identify themselves with the less, and not the more, gifted. And we get some clue to the reason from the mouth of a man who has been called the last man of the ancient world, the last Roman, a Pope, St. Gregory the Great, when he writes that the doctrine of human inequality springs *ex fonte superbiae*, "from the fount of pride"—not only a snobbery but a cardinal sin, and one held by the Church to be among the closest to the original sin of obstinate and distrustful self-will. Many people lose in the struggle for success and glittering prizes, not because they lack virtue or morality or even ability but because they remain more attached to duty and its ties and loyalties, which others desert in order to tread on the fingers of their fellows as they climb the worldly ladder. There would seem, then, to be more to the Doctrine of Equality than is known to science. And we find indeed no other than President Eisenhower placing it again among the fundamental moral convictions of the West. "The brotherhood of man is God-given and enduring."

The fundamental principle at stake, one may suspect, is not that of egalitarianism, unless by this be merely meant 'equality before the law' or 'equality of opportunity,' or repudiation of false inequalities, or religious reflection upon the unimportance of external inequalities when it comes to divine judgement of the naked man—men all equally children and nothing but God's creatures. *The fundamental principle at stake is rather that of Fraternity. What is required is Fraternity for All and Equality of opportunity for Each.* The notion of equality is derivative from 'the one spirit' of brotherhood. The lust for private power and dominion destroys it. *Deposuit potentes,* says *Magnificat.* "He hath exalted the humble." If a child falls into a river we do not pause to ask whether it be Englishman, Dutchman or Dago, Mongol or piccaninny, of Brahmin or *sudra* caste. If this term, fraternity, is sometimes avoided, although more exact, it is from fear perhaps that a man's independence may be sapped if, behind the cloak of fraternity, there lurks elder brother patronage.

The sentiment of fraternity is not something deducible from scientific surveys, although a pseudo-science which tried to prevent it, as "not Darwinian," can be demolished by more exact science. Rather it is a religious and indeed theological principle of faith, which yet has support sociological and psychological. The practising denial of fraternity breaks up (as Mr. C. A. R. Crosland has recently written in *Encounter*) the community of the society, of civilization, of humanity itself; and opens the gates, all too technically easy to open, through hardening of men's hearts, to the Gadarene rush to race destruction.

Men are indeed deeply individual persons, with souls and minds of their own, sometimes good haters, as well as social members. Power through the ages has always inclined its possessors to disregard or condemn that human fact which is so administratively inconvenient. It is easier to say, with Halifax 'the Trimmer', that to govern men "they must be treated scurvily."

Were it true, as some philosophical anarchists suppose, that men are naturally cooperative, we could leave the matter there with the bare assertion that all men are persons. But it is not so, The psychoanalyst is aware that the human soul, although naturally good in innocence, is divided. And although education and an authentic propaganda can always appeal to the side that trusts, there is a side with an original bias, in the very affirmation of the self, to distrust, suspicion, fear, confirmed as hate. There lies, as Freud said, the deep menace, native in the soul of every single man, Russian, Prussian or American, to civilization itself. And although much distrust can be educated away, some species of anti-fraternity present such a danger to society that they must at need be demolished by force.

In the interest of society itself, such 'uncivilization' is literally intolerable. There are indeed small communities, homogeneous in values, which can seek to be exclusive. They can talk about national survival and, with Hitler, about race purity. But their legitimate claims—and the claims of community can be legitimate—must yet be vigorously subordinated to those of man himself and of the wider community.

3

The Race issue, as one expression of the fight about human equality and fraternity, is one of the most crucial for those who aspire to moral leadership in the world, but one in which the West still makes an imperfect showing. Here Soviet propaganda still has an edge, the edge on us. On the one side stands the enunciation of great principles, from Lord Mansfield to the Supreme Court of the United States. On the other side has to be placed—to go no further—the actual conduct of people in parts of British Africa and of the Southern United States.

Not to speak of India, Burma and Ceylon, the British record in the Caribbean, Nigeria and the Gold Coast will stand up, as creditable, under examination—nor in these latter cases is there question of shortage of finance or military power as being decisive in a policy which was indeed settled by the electorate for broader and more liberal reasons. In the United Kingdom the introduction of Negroes from Jamaica or West Africa into the railway and postal services, as a matter of policy, is highly creditable. (Maybe some day there will be legislation penalizing, for government contracts, employers and unions who practice a 'colour bar'.) It has not always been easy. This credit, however, largely belongs to the metropolitan Government.

It is yet not enough to claim that a regime of liberty, democracy and respect for human rights exists at home. Responsibility cannot be disclaimed for what happens in what are unhappily called 'the Overseas Possessions,' or even for what happens in sovereign sections of what still remains the Commonwealth. As Mr. James Cameron, of the *News Chronicle*, has written in an article 'When We Lift the Lid in Kenya':

"Elsewhere this fine progress has not only come to a halt, but is actually reverting to a Victorian condition of blackjack domination. When the worst of the Nazi excesses were exposed, Germany, if you recall, resounded to the protestations of Germans who 'hadn't known what was going on,' who 'never had been told.' We British have no such terrible secret in our midst, but things have been, and are, going on outside that are not incomparable. What is more, we know. Come judgement day, not one of us here can plead ignorance when the whole tale of Kenya and Cyprus is on the record for any sort of analysis. That is the thing [in Nigeria and Kenya] of which British people may feel simultaneously proud and ashamed—or, in other words, normal."

White planters have got to recognize that if they persist in a policy of repression and weighted justice, the day will surely come when, as in Haiti, they will be murdered in their beds by an exasperated and immensely preponderant people, or, should there be a war which the Soviets win, they will be strung up from the nearest trees. Nor can the liberal West afford, whatever may be the Ulster-like and strictly conditioned loyalty of these planters (and military men have not failed to warn some that the accents of this loyalty sounded more like treason), to give support and commitment to this reaction.

They can, of course, turn to South Africa. A British Liberal Cabinet must be held blameworthy, knowing the traditional and fervently-held Boer racial tradition which caused the *trek* to the Transvaal, for not having insisted, after military victory, upon a Constitution which enacted a full Bill of Rights; entrenched a Supreme Court; and provided for a developing electorate, such as would prevent permanent minority rule. The damage, through excess of optimism, has now been done.

Nor is it helpful to underestimate the strength of the Boer case. In fighting against distant British pressure and present Negro demands, they claim that they are fighting for national survival as a pure race. However, they have in principle their remedy—which they refuse to take. They can *trek* again. The South Africans, unlike the white Australians, seem to have no intention of working their own lands and mines with white manual labour.

The economic development of South Africa, unless the Afrikanders are prepared to cultivate a small area of the present land as an agricultural settlement for themselves, will inevitably decide that ultimately the Negro must be brought into partnership, if not into formal control. If to-day he sits in rags, that is not because rags alone become him, but because his abler young men are not allowed to develop and because, so far as economically can be done, rags and low wages alone are permitted to him. Fraternity is being nauseatingly interpreted as "telling the nigger to mind his place," of course for his own good; and, under a system of no determinate spiritual authority, it is even being odiously and indeed blasphemously declared that this is to be called a Christian State system. It is, of course, a Nazi system.

In the Southern United States slowly the system changes so that, if two generations of time are permitted, vast transformations can take place. There is not here the complication of the immense reservoir of Negro manpower that exists on the borders of South Africa. The trouble here does not lie with the Southern aristocrats. It is courageous Southern judges of this type who have administered the law, to their immeasurable credit, strictly according to their oath. In one case a Southern judge, Judge Waring, declared that "he no more gave the Negro anything that was not his under the Constitution than, by restoring his watch to a man who had had his stolen, one gave him a new watch."

At least the Catholic Church in the South, from St. Louis to New Orleans, has here written for itself a splendid record. It was the Rector of a New Orleans Catholic school who declared that segregation was "un-Christian, un-Catholic and un-American."

Truth is an antiseptic, which pains in the poisoned parts. The opposition comes in large measure from backward and rural areas, from economic jealousy and from those who have little to boast about save the colour of their skin, and from those whom a conservative President of the United States described to the present writer as "poor white trash." What is required is the general improvement of economic conditions, which will end a trashy situation, and even bolder white leadership in the South, both aristocratic and trades union. Up to date, as one eminent journalist has pointed out, the Catholic Church is doing a much better job here than the trades union leadership. The gentlemen and the law must have the courage to tell the hoodlums 'where they get off'. To do this, however, the law must have force and power.

There are some people, of course, who will not learn, but have their faces set to a more comfortable past of their own imagination, flattering to their power, an expurgated past. The actual past, in this issue, displays three cases of military defeat and two of unconditional surrender.

In the United States, no one desires that Sherman shall march again through Georgia—but the doctrine of 'State Interposition' can yet threaten the integrity of the Union.

Just as 'the Yellow Peril' recalls the Kaiser Wilhelm, so in South Africa, the doctrine of *apartheid* tends to be practically indistinguishable from Hitler's *Rassentheorie*. With the Hitlerite ideology it had its chance. Too many people forget that Hitler is dead, and that this campaign ended in crushing military defeat and, like the campaign of the South, in unconditional surrender, just as the campaign of the Boers ended in defeat.

It is pleasanter to forget these things. But it may be too easy. On the other side, there are those who maliciously ignore what has already been done in the South, who ignore the great progress made and the courage of the Southerners—men such as Graham of Chapel Hill—who have withstood embattled ignorance in order to make that progress. Their names will be remembered, as said Nehemiah, for good.

4

No sane man would suggest that the racial issue is something uncomplicated, to be settled by simple principles. It may be that the future of the white man in Africa is to be found in conducting himself as the Jews have always done, and in living by his wits, his superior intelligence and organizing and fiscal ability. Not who has the government but who has the commercial know-how, the wealth, may be the test. The Negro on the whole is an amiable human being, "of a free and open nature," more amiable than most; but he is not equally a well-controlled human being. And with every depressed people it must be expected that, when it is given its head, certain excesses will result to which the sociologist must attend and for which wise statesmanship will allow. Much, indeed almost everything, depends upon the human capacity, granted benevolence, for change (in which, for example, the Capricorn Society, in Central Africa, puts its trust); upon equal opportunity for men of ability of any colour; on respect for the rights of all rational human beings as such, including the right to be educated; and on the promotion of the rights of civilized human beings, as Rhodes said.

There is indeed the problem of miscegenation, although this is not felt to be such, e.g. in Brazil. It would be a poor sociology which overlooked that even the impoverished, segregationist whites have their case.

We can regard race mixture, even if usually undesirable, as very much a matter of individual choice. Many people, on both sides, will not want to mix. No one should compel them. Broadly the negro and mulatto aspire to marry those more white than themselves. They should not be discouraged individually, however unwise it may be in practice as an indiscriminate rule. About racial intermarriage in Asia there has seldom been much difficulty except, for caste reasons, among Asians themselves. National exogamy has its attractions. Racial intermixture is "either non-U or super-U." Either it takes place at the highest aristocratic levels where only culture counts, not nationality; or it occurs where there are few social controls. The maximum resentment against it comes from people of the social level of Hitler himself. It is a lower middle-class phenomenon, where a rather vulgar insensitivity about human values moralistically parades itself as high sensitivity. It is also a declining phenomenon.

Human beings are indeed unequal, but the valid distinctions follow other lines. It is because some inferior-feeling people sense this, and that the judgement may be against themselves, in an aristocracy, that they cling to such obvious matters as a colour-bar, at whatever cost.

What matters is not the colour of people's skin but the degree of their capacity for partaking in high civilization. The Chinese patently have such a capacity, on the record more than some Europeans. Maybe some Negroes will prove not to have it; we do not know yet. Some Negroes have high musical gifts and a natural personal dignity which to-day the 'democratic' West tends to under-value. Not all white people have this capacity. Some are vulgarian. The water must find its own level. But for the present, aided by friendly cultural surroundings, we must preserve the *carrière ouverte aux talents*, 'equality of opportunity,' taken in no narrow intellectualist sense. And the secret of providing such fostering surroundings is the inculcation of the charitable sense of fraternity.

This is not a superficial issue. It is one of the basic issues— perhaps it is the *basic issue in charity—of our civilization, and quite peculiarly of any Christian civilization.*

De-segregation does not mean that superior intelligence, ability and standards must yield before a lower culture. It means the precise opposite, that lower standards must yield to superior intelligence, dignity, morality and gifts *wherever* these may be found. This is true individualism as well as sound sociality. But it is not a matter which individuals or local groups can be left, in a modern society, free by their prejudices to decide for others. The issue is one of national interest and security.

If the free world is unable to clarify its own mind on this ancient issue then it will perish before Soviet propaganda. And, moreover, it will deserve to perish. There are indeed moral values and moral distinctions. But those who oppose fraternity, irrespective of such moral evaluations—not because people are of different values, but because they are black—are quite precisely 'enemies of the human race.'

The Free World, including the West, has shared in a liberal and human tradition for which, although compromised by Soviet demands in the Baltic, Poland, Hungary and elsewhere, it fought successfully against Hitler. But, in this Twentieth Century, it would be quite wrong to suppose that the victory of liberalism (and here in its English, not its Continental, sense) will be gradual perhaps but yet inevitable. Its victory will depend upon our own courage in inscribing the Jeffersonian ideals of the Declaration of Independence on our banners and carrying them forward, not unaware of the criticism but convinced of the cause.

VI

THE FREE COMMONWEALTH

1

HITHERTO we have been concerned to discuss, not abstract political goals in some ideal world, but the kind of things that have generally been accepted as political aims; the language of priorities as touching these aims; the kind of declarations that have to be made if a large part of the human race is not to prefer the ostensible policies of the Soviet Union as 'progressive' to those of the West—and, not least, what we have got to accept in the way of change if we are, in fact, to achieve our own required ends.

Everybody in politics, as in business, would prefer to be the possessor of splendid goods for which no payments were required. But one of the incidental advantages of the science of politics is to demonstrate to us quite clearly that, in this field also, nothing is to be had for nothing. This is, of course, an unpleasant conclusion. In this chapter I want to outline *the direction and conditions of peaceful change*, such as will assure the maintenance of peace for those peoples who think that they also understand and love liberty and justice— restressing that peaceful change is liable to be about as painful as a surgical operation.

We can, of course, be met at the outset with the contention that 'the public' will not tolerate such an operation. The answer to this is simple: 'If so, the public will probably end by being vaporized into inflammable hydrogen gas.' There is no evidence that to-day, whoever may be the victor, a major war can be waged without vast destruction of life; and every minor war, even a Balkan or Middle Eastern one, has to be viewed from the angle of its likelihood of extending into a major war.

'Public opinion' is not something which springs up rather as the men of the legend are supposed to have sprung up, fully armed when the dragons' teeth were sown. Public opinion is guided, shaped and made; and, if public opinion is intransigent and reactionary, it is because the leaders of opinion and men of ideas have been cowardly and have not been doing their job. The judgement of the common man, and even of members of Parliament and Senators, is not by predestination irrational and reactionary.

Some years ago Mr. Lowes Dickinson, in commenting on 'the International Anarchy,' and later Lord Lothian, in his justly famous Burge Lecture, pointed out that peace is quite incompatible with preserving the doctrine of absolute national or local sovereignty, any more than peace would be preserved in the United States were the sovereignty of Texas or Virginia accepted (for accepted it is) in more than a very modified and restricted sense. This new view was proclaimed explicitly at the time of the San Francisco Conference, even in unexpected quarters, by such statesmen as Mr. T. V. Soong of China and Mr. Jan Hofmeyer of South Africa and later, in more general terminology, by Mr. Ernest Bevin, Sir Anthony Eden and Mr. Harold Macmillan.

Oddly enough it has been generals, who are usually regarded as the especial champions of national claims, who have been busiest in making affirmation of the need for a new look. Two great wars were each fought by coordinated armies under an international general, Foch and Eisenhower; and no one has been busier than Field Marshal Viscount Montgomery in campaigning for a NATO army and an international air force. The generals face facts. The local orators tend to evade them, in favour of tribal or clan emotions which produce votes.

Instead of the analogy, used above, of a surgical operation, a more apt one could be that of the replacement of archaic machinery by new—a process which yet can be almost equally painful to those accustomed to earlier positions of prestige as proud tenders of these museum pieces.

The system of sovereign states grew up with the New Monarchies in the Sixteenth Century, but was so far *parvenu* as not to develop a self-confident theory of itself until the close of the century and indeed until the Seventeenth Century. Even the great lawyer Blackstone here wavers, in his jurisprudence, between incompatibilities.

The fusion, moreover, of the system of the sovereign state—as offering to its subjects peace and security better than the old feudal manorial system (so suited to local defence) of lord and vassal—with the sentiment of popular national loyalty did not precede Danton and the French Revolution. At the beginning of the last century it was still repudiated by Metternich.

The system and theory of state sovereignty evolved at a given point in history to perform a function. The system is no more an essential or inevitability of politics than feudalism. The function was to maintain a domestic peace in better fashion than the baronial system could any longer do, without yet abolishing local government; and to obtain in relation with other realms the assurance of peace or victory. Owing to technological developments which make most national states less self-sufficient, *this function the sovereign states shaped in the Seventeenth Century, as a matter of machinery, can no longer to-day perform.*

On the other hand, technological developments in the arts of war make the need for the efficient performance of the function of peace-keeping (victory being to-day of a Pyrrhic quality) ever more urgent in popular demand. The older warning of Rome and of Dante that the *pax mundi* requires massive unity and indeed a kind of World Government becomes more patently commonsense.

112

One route out, which we reject, would be a world tyranny by conquest, under the Kremlin or Potsdam. The Kremlin is *not* of course the only contemporary tyranny; but it is the only one with power to menace, except in the indirect and practical way open, for example, to the controller of some great commercial sea way. Another route, to which some statesmen seem to lean, is just to go on as before in diplomatic anarchy hoping that the sheer terror and fear of hydrogen explosion will keep the peace, in a world where (as Sir Anthony Eden said) if war comes then bombs, unlike poison gas, will be used. It is rash to trust to a chance which some day may chance not to prevent the descent from the skies of a final judgement in the twinkling of an eye, like lightning from the east, and the burying of civilization under lethal ash.

In connection with the Suez Canal dispute, it is perhaps not remarkable that Mr. Aneurin Bevan should say that "all nations must be prepared to accept some diminution of their sovereign rights if the world is to become friendlier and more closely knit." But it is noteworthy that the British Foreign Secretary, Mr. Selwyn Lloyd, has indeed developed a most interesting, certainly novel—and even bold—doctrine of sovereignty. Whereas it is stated that the Egyptian Government has "full sovereign ownership" of the Canal, the "administration as well as control" of the Canal would lie with an "international" or rather a multinational body—a theme which could provide a highly significant precedent for other international waterways, air strips, etc.   Mr. Selwyn Lloyd, at the London Suez Conference, said:

"it has been inferred outside this Conference that international participation in the control or operation of the Suez Canal would be an infringement of Egyptian sovereignty. I do not accept that proposition . . . That view, I submit, is based on a complete misconception of the nature of sovereignty under international law. Sovereignty does not mean the right to do exactly what you please within your own territory."

And indeed Colonel Nasser should be the last person to advocate a conception of nationalism and Austinian sovereigty, the will of the nation being absolute, complete and final, such as would entitle the Sudan Government to divert to its own purposes the waters of the Nile. Even the Rhine and Danube navigation has been regulated in accord with more international concepts; and the same views might perchance hold for the Panama Canal (as Mr. Harry S. Truman has recently admitted), Dardanelles, Straits of Gibraltar, Aden and St. Lawrence, although of course each has its own difficulties. One useful technique of approach here might be to establish a multinational High Authority to deal functionally and specifically with oil and its transport, not as touching Egyptian waters alone and hence not involving issues of Arab or Egyptian sovereignty alone.

At no point are the conclusions of political science more unambiguous than here in its analysis of power. Yet popular demand is confused by the very proper emotions of national loyalty, which have swept Europe and are to-day sweeping Asia with consequences that we all know.

A hopeful element lies in the historical fact that, in Asia (as in Europe with Mazzini and Victor Hugo), such great national leaders as Mohandas Gandhi, *pater patriae*, have also been leading voices and visionaries in proclaiming the duties of internationalism. Also, England and even the United Kingdom have found it impossible to grow as political entities solely on the principle of tribal nationality, which has given way to the multi-national and multi-racial principle of the Commonwealth; and instead of the local States of the American Union, there has been accepted with enthusiasm the principle of a continental Union, "our Federal Union strong and free," based rather on immigration than on nationality by blood.

One goal, therefore, if we desire civil peace, is to reform the machinery that it may better perform its function under Twentieth Century conditions. To this end, we must encourage by votes and support those modern and competent engineers who seek increasingly to substitute international machinery *with authority*—without thereby discarding altogether the national and *staatlich* organizations, any more than the national states, in their time, discarded the more elemental instruments of the face-to-face community in local government.

It will not, however, surprise us if the opposition to this efficiency is likely chiefly to come from those Powers still Great, which are therefore nearly enough self-sufficient to enable the old-fangled system to seem to work—to wit, Germany and Japan until yesterday, Russia and, let us add, the United States and Great Britain, under a Conservative government, just in so far as it is part of a vast Commonwealth, whether it consults that Commonwealth or (as recently) not. Truly great statesmanship, while keeping its feet on the ground and, like Napoleon, attending to detail, yet always ascends to those heights which more timid and incompetent spirits dismiss as 'merely visionary.' So Sir Winston Churchill, possibly on the prompting of M. Monnet, made his offer of union to France and indeed went so far that alarmed persons, such as Mr. Warbey, in the House of Commons sought (without success) to extract a binding promise from him not to make the same offer to the United States.

Some would urge that individual natural rights, political democracy as understood in the Anglo-Saxon world at least, and international federation with state rights are so logically connected as to be one philosophical argument. This federal union case raises too great controversy for discussion here. It may well be academically sound; but politically it crosses many bridges before the rivers have been reached. A less frontal approach is wiser.

This writer has consistently urged that case for Organic Union, involving discussions and interchange of plans and personnel, which statement Mr. Walter Lippmann was good enough to quote as part of U.S. War Aim One, in his book *U.S. War Aims*. Sir Robert Boothby, M.P., has been not the least of its champions. It has been the course followed by those statesmen of post-war Europe, Robert Schuman, Conrad Adenauer and Alcide de Gasperi, and it has issued, under the advice and expertise of MM. Monnet and Uri, in the Steel and Coal High Authority in Luxembourg—which these gentlemen have made quite plain is *not* merely 'functional' but has political implications—and in Euratom, a Continental scheme for the peaceful use of atomic power which puts the British economists and politicians squarely 'on the spot.'

Statesmanship will consist in arming the United Nations as of old the Sheriff was armed in affairs of the civil peace, with 'a big stick' to maintain world peace, bigger than that of any law-breaker or underworld character whatsoever, with practical atomic monopoly for this function—just as, in the end, the King of France was able to call to order the Duke of Burgundy. As General Maxwell Taylor, U.S. Army Chief of Staff, said recently, it is quite wrong to suppose that the era of local aggression and small wars, requiring manpower, is ended—and, as First World War experience shows, these even by miscalculation can become global. If, however, the veto be regarded as irremovable from the United Nations Organisation, so that its executive power is staggered, then the big stick must be wielded by the Free World Commonwealth on behalf of the United Nations, according to the principles of conduct which they may, by Assembly majority, approve. A certain healthy obstinacy of State rights can still remain. The power-house of action, to change the metaphor, for the moment remains the Washington-Westminster-Ottawa triangle, while the legislative 'sense of the meeting' is to be found in the United Nations.

Statesmanship will declare, with Sir Winston Churchill recently, that our purpose must be to maintain law, order and, as a rigid and unvarying instruction, the Anglo-American Alliance (not the Triple Entente), with organic consultation therein, concomitantly with the entire Commonwealth, as a routine matter. It is perhaps regrettable that the Franco-Russian link of the Triple Entente still remains as a treaty obligation, whereas no like bilateral obligations in law tie the United States with either Britain or France. In the words of President Eisenhower, in Convention Hall, Philadelphia, there yet "can be no second-class nations before the law of the world community . . . There can be only one law, or there will be no peace". "The peace we seek and need means much more than mere absence of war. It means the acceptance of law and the fostering of justice in all the world".

Indeed, in building up the United Nations, we have to decide whether it is *it* or *we*, as judge and plaintiff, which is to decide how its power is to be built up. Here the remark of M. Pineau, of France, is (even if unintentionally) relevant. He said on November 14, 1956, adverting to Egypt : "In an international organization you cannot have two different rules". The U.N., he said, should be just as severe with one set of nations as with another, dictatorial or democratic. It is 'the law and the King's peace', not that of duke or baron, which must prevail. But, no less, the king must not be *fainéant*. For the moment the United Nations have two mayors of the palace, the Kremlin and the Atlantic Alliance so far as it is ratified in policy by an Assembly majority. The West, and the East, must choose—maybe between evils, maybe between goods. Peace depends ultimately upon the Unbalance of Power, not upon the tempting, by balance, of aggression into a gamble.

We must avoid the cold-foot defeatism which, sometime advocating neutrality in Germany or Central Europe, and sometime discouraging the very hope of liberation from military tyranny in Eastern Europe, holds (as sometimes does Mr. Lippmann) that it is no function of any United Nations tribunal or high court to be a court of judgement. On the contrary, any policy at all presupposes, not only some scientific 'solution', but a judgement. Here the head has lost faith in man and, by diplomatic calculations of false realism, chills the heart. It is those who have held the opposite who have memorably contributed by heroism to human dignity in our times.

Admittedly, we must concede two points to critics of the United Nations. First, the present United Nations machinery can provide a cruel hoax for those who imagine that it is *already* equipped of itself to maintain the peace. The history of nations, of the sentiment of world community, and of international law, is in process of evolution. Those, indeed, are most swift to point this out who themselves seem most reluctant to improve it by modifying the veto, by giving the Assembly power to do more than recommend, and by making the military clause of the Charter operative. They do not with faith work for improvement but with a reactionary pseudo-realism, which can end in disaster, look back to the anarchy, qualified by occasional balance, of the past. The notion of the pre-established harmonious balance of the Great Powers as even approximately automatic is historic nonsense, mistaking a lull before the storm for fair weather.

Secondly, let us be clear that, as has been known since the days of the Pharisees, strict and formal legalism, for example in rigid definitions of aggression, can do great injustice and prevent peaceful and evolutionary change as well as revolutionary struggles for freedom. However, in the history of the evolution of law, such formalism in securing respect for the processes of law precedes the refinements of justice through equity. We must be patient with the imperfections of evolving organizations. At least justice must not be self-defined by the plaintiffs and its name taken in vain. In the argument of Kant, strictly there is no just war whilst the plaintiff sits on the judge's bench to adjudicate upon what is just.

What yet is intolerable is to have a world organization for peace and justice so imperfect that it can stigmatize an aggression but has itself neither legislature, competent to redefine the *status quo* with change of circumstance, nor executive, to see that a doer of injustice is actually penalized. Great Powers cannot be expected to tolerate this species of incompetent humiliation, although they may bow to an effective *force majeure* determined to impose law and order. Nevertheless, the Great Powers severally and individually are no longer competent, even to the small degree that they once were in the days of the Holy Alliance, to keep this peace.

The case here is that, whatever way we should go, the old state sovereignty system, economically no less than politically, is in the words of Mr. R. F. Harrod "an outmoded concept." It would be politically unwise to say that the sovereignty even of Texas should be 'abolished.' What must be asserted is that the days of sovereignty, as understood by the great jurist Austin, are over and that state sovereignty must increasingly be 'pooled.' *What will emerge will (in the case of Steel and Coal) as with the High Authority itself, be sovereign,* in the context of its own functional competence and of the emergent European constitutional morality.

However we have not reached this stage yet. England has ceased to be sovereign; the Commonwealth never was; but the United Kingdom is sovereign—and, let us repeat, in its own proper functional field, is likely to remain such.

2

The present writer, on the other hand, in a series of books, *The History of the Political Philosophers*, *The Anglo-Saxon Tradition* and another with the sub-title of *The Foundations of*

Anglo-Saxony—learning from that very great teacher and League of Nations statesman, Professor Gilbert Murray, that "sovereignty can only be pooled by those who share values"—has sought to establish as balance to the above schemes of mechanical and institutional change, the concept of a cultural tradition. Here I mean both a Grand Tradition of humanity (which Sir Ernest Barker calls 'Traditions of Civility') and, within this Humanism, a more local and empiric tradition characteristic of the English-speaking peoples and especially binding the great Western Republic with the more Eastern parts of *les Pouvoirs Anglo-Saxonnes* (the habitual Continental identification) in the United Kingdom.

It is by no means the theme of this book that sovereign national states are just to be regarded (as the Webbs sometimes did) as pocket-handkerchief areas of administrative convenience or inconvenience, or as pieces of power machinery to be changed by bureaucrats for some New Model—not that the drastic New Model of Cromwell's Commonwealth was a thing to be despised. There are common values alike of Realm and Republic; there are (it is my faith) common values of the Anglo-Saxon world, as also of Europe; there are common values of high civilization in the whole round globe. Pakistani and Indonesian also have this sense of national values. In so far as it presents an obstacle to international rearrangements, this spiritual sentiment is not something that, in the abstract spirit of 1789, can just be brusquely treated or disregarded.

The late Wendell L. Willkie, one of the most remarkable of recent American figures, advocated *both* 'one world' *and* a social and economic union of the United States and the British Commonwealth, as sharing common values, with free migration and interchangeable citizenship. I had the honour of knowing something of Mr. Willkie's hopes and, in my *One Anglo-Amercian Nation*, written in the mental climate of these hopes and of Mr. Churchill's offer to France, I outlined a sober project of shared plans, as an organic and not an exceptional procedure, which received, if I may say so with modesty, some little approbation in responsible quarters and which indeed Lord Chancellor Sankey over-praised by saying that it "deserved well of two hemispheres." I have at all times and unashamedly been a profound believer, if in humanism and man, yet also in North American man. These proposals can now (perhaps unfortunately) be regarded as quite dead. They do yet live as the project of the Atlantic Community. And here is the only adequate focus of power for the United Kingdom, which is indeed a mere Sweden without its Commonwealth.

It is well to bear in mind that, however bright (as some of us ardently hope) may be the prospects of effective Western European Union, industrial or otherwise, with a Common Market, and however weighty and stable may or may not be the collaboration of Bonn (or Berlin) after Adenauer with Paris after Schuman and Mollet, nevertheless the power house of the West remains the triangle Washington-Westminster-Ottawa.

Further, if the over-crowded island of Great Britain is not for ever to tighten its belt in domestic consumption and the home market, in the interests of an everlasting pursuit of competitive exports at competitive labor costs, it must enter a free trade and common market area. And it is entirely to its advantage that this area shall not, as with Europe, be one in which its own people not only produce most, man for man, by machine aids (as it still does) but also expect more than the rest expect—so that free trade and free migration can mean levelling *down*. It is to its advantage to be part of a prosperous common area of high standards where its levelling will be levelling *up*. Nor (as the recent case of Iceland shows) can the United States be uninterested politically outside its own borders.

Recently, in 1956, (although this is little known) Denmark explored the possibility of joining the British Commonwealth. Surprised British statesmen could give no reply. Such union has even been talked of by spokesmen from Israel. But these unions can be brought to birth—and it is an error to imagine they do not enter the area of practical politics. Thirty years ago Mr. Bruce, Premier of Australia, later Lord Bruce of Melbourne, proposed that when the Imperial Conference met in Ottawa the United States should be invited to send observers, an invitation which the Administration of President Calvin Coolidge most short-sightedly rejected.

To use the older terms, the power-house is the United States and the British Commonwealth, with its lines stretching out to Sydney but also still to Delhi. In one sense it can prove a great source of weakness that the British Empire was so polyglot and multiracial, far more so than the old Hapsburg Empire. We do well to unite with those who share our accustomed way of life in lands of our own speech. In another sense English is a world language and it is not our disadvantage, but our great good fortune, that our citizenship crosses all colour and racial bars. *Here is both idealism and power.* Indeed the connection with Delhi is to-day not that of a lien on a bright jewel in a crown imperial, but a tie with a seventh of humanity which demonstrates beyond debate that the Commonwealth is no *apartheid* racial block.

We have, then, to bear in mind that our task is not only to modify the machinery of government so that, instead of the crushing economic burden of contemporary state defence forces, we can establish a system that functions more efficiently to assure peace. We also, in carrying through this change (and here has lain the error of some impatient blueprint reformers), have got to make allowance for the traditions and sentiments of peoples great and small. The case in Europe may be most weighty for a common market with mobility of labour; but we have to bear in mind that the other name for the abstraction 'mobility of labour' is *the rootlessness of men and women, for whom their attachment to their local community is among the most valuable and desirable things that they possess and the substance of civic virtue.* We can compromise and adjust in political science; but we cannot have it fully both ways. There is a political law of choice.

Sometimes a new nation has been born almost entirely from a profound sentiment of attachment to the values of language and tradition, as with Czecho-Slovakia; or to a religion, as with Israel and Pakistan. Unlike the French, the intellectual leaders of the Anglo-Saxon peoples grossly underestimate the political importance of language. It may well be that five centuries hence England, like Rome, will only be recalled in terms of its world language and its laws.

Sometimes, however, a new State can be set up which itself engenders a new sentiment, as with the United Kingdom itself, thanks to determined men who unblushingly pushed through the unpopular change by bribery and corruption with cash and honours, with no nonsense about following a laggard public opinion.

An Atlantic Union will doubtless be achieved by both methods; and, in so far as European Union has been achieved, it has been by resolute statesmen first achieving a stranglehold on the key sectors of the European economy, and then menacing the civil servants of the various European national Treasuries and Foreign Offices that they will be brought into the courts of the sovereign High Authority as treaty-breakers if they prevaricate.

This is strong meat. It is also one of the great historic events of this disturbed decade. Patently, however, the situation is most satisfactory if we can rely, as perhaps in Europe or the Commonwealth, upon a sufficently strong sentiment of common values, aroused by inspired intellectual leadership, for the political transition to be carried through without pain. A strong new hope can provide anaesthesia.

The difficulty, in the case of the United Nations, is that, without a great resurgence of world-wide humanism, emotion is here most diffuse, thin-spread and at a minimum. Some will seek to evade this difficulty by the suggestion that the international authority should be functional and limited only to the work of international arbitration and police force, just as the European High Authority at Luxemburg was for steel and coal. The whole history, however, of the High Authority and the specific declaration of M. Robert Schuman indicate that, however prudent this approach may be (as it is) as a tactic, in the last resort the political issue of who holds the superior sovereignty has to be confronted. The moral is that *we must prepare public opinion* for these great changes. In the United States the position is too often (despite the admirable lead given by some American citizens and in the resolutions of fourteen State legislatures) that these changes are greatly favoured so long as they are strictly confined to other people . . .

3

Regional integrations, such as Western Europe, provide vehicles of common values, for which men of vision have worked such as Coudenhove-Kalergi, not to speak of Victor Hugo and, in our own days, Briand, Schuman, Adenauer and also Churchill. They provide a useful synthesis of community sentiment with international integration, breaking down of frontiers and fusion of peoples. Western Europe becomes the modern political expression of the Carolingian idea. It is licit within the terms of the United Nations Charter. But, as an instrument for the function of maintaining peace and indeed increasing prosperity by the decrease of defence costs, it raises certain new problems. Do not European or Atlantic or Common-wealth or Soviet Communist bloc unions threaten the world with a danger to peace—not only making ' all wars world wars', as was said of the League of Nations and United Nations, but dividing the world into armed camps? What the philosopher Kant said was crucial, to wit that, without a World Court of adequate powers, we are not entitled to say of any punitive action that it is 'just' or of any aggressor that he is identified. It is an observation worth pondering.

Here we require to preserve our historic sense. The impartial police force develops from the rough justice of the sheriff's posse. Even Mr. Gandhi admitted to this writer that, could one get an entirely impartial world court *and* police force, it should be supported.

World courts evolve as have the King's courts. In the history of law much justice and identification of agressors have been political. Not for nothing did the great Emperor Justinian, introducing his Code, say that he held authority 'by arms and laws.' Indeed Natural Law is basic; but its understanding and interpretation evolve. We must accept power blocs. But the conscience of humanity will be satisfied by that power bloc which more patently, and by its propaganda more convincingly, shows that it is indeed concerned to build a world organization for enforcing the rule of a developing law, in cooperation with all men of goodwill who do themselves cooperate.

We may, therefore, doubt the power actually to enforce peace of self-proclaimed international forums (not as yet universal) which are not even like-minded clubs. This does not mean that international debates and cooperation in neutral spheres are not invaluable, or that the United Nations should be scrapped, instead of reformed. Through them, subtler instruments of pressure can be shaped. We ought to build an international police as effective instrument of a world law, which must itself evolve and not be too legalistic lest *summumius* be *summa iniuria*. We can, however, with clear conscience welcome defensive and positive integrations such as

Europe or the Atlantic or Commonwealth Unions, from which can spring new and genuine policies.

Does this concretely mean that NATO should be supported in order that, at need, in the interests of stable law and peace, expansive tyrannies, with which we do not share values, shall be put under heel or 'cut down to size'? Despite the lesson of 1936, pointing to the occasional need for preventive war or like action. I see no reason to adopt this aggressive phraseology. The ultimate instrument of peace must be world-wide, although capable of 'enforcing peace' and of punishing all local rebellion and resort to force. The present instruments, being partial, are also relative in expediency and in process of evolution. We cannot brandish a weapon in weak provocation, as before Munich, or until the arm behind it is muscular. Their task is simply to render expansion by tyranny unprofitable and the promotion of whatever true values may be found in any quarter made, by the free circulation of ideas, more likely.

The task of these organizations is to show that their own positive plans, through the breaking down of frontiers, are concretely successful, so that others may seek to imitate, not tyranny, but liberty. Their object should be to make liberty also strong, and peace the associate of justice and liberty.

4

There are some people who present the problem of this chapter as one of alternatives: whether to support the United Nations or Atlantic Union or European Union or national self-sufficiency. They argue that one cannot urge upon the electorate a little of this and a little of that. I submit that this is an entirely false presentation of the issue. We should support everything that tends realistically to our assigned goal. Only the occasion can decide what, in a given situation, presents most opportunity.

Our symbol or analogy should not be of choice between

three or more political models, but of a Chinese 'box' or cabinet, each containing smaller ones which compatibly fit into it. Within the framework of the United Nations fits the Atlantic Community, which (unlike the clumsy NATO machine) should not exclude Australasia or any part whatsoever of the Commonwealth; and within the integrated Atlantic Community should fit the European union of the six or more countries, which should be less in extension but even more intensively a community of values, and more integrated.

It is absurd to ask: Should North America join a United Europe? Should, then, the United Kingdom, without Canada, join a United Europe? One is tempted to reply that (reserving the field of agriculture) within ten years the United Kingdom will have to, or be crushed. For centuries England has profited, in the name of liberty, by the disunion of Europe and balance of power. With the union of a free Europe that 'splendid isolation' has now come finally to an end. But actually I would give another reply.

Our goal, beyond the United Nations (primarily an association of victor states), is a world Commonwealth of Free Nations. *We have to make this so strong that the Soviet will join it on free terms, the terms of that Free Commonwealth* springing from the earlier work of League of Nations and United Nations—although not on the terms of *apartheid* or free-for-all exploitation or any such local 'ism.' European Union is to be welcomed and forwarded in so far as it is regarded as a part, perhaps never to be matured in isolation, of a wider plan, a box within a bigger box, maybe the box of the moment. It is competent to frighten the reactionary by its potential power. As against the illusion of national self-sufficiency, it deserves the support of courageous men. But as some kind of Middle Way or Third Bloc, itself self-sufficient, it does not merit support. It has neither the emotion of the old nor the realism of the new.

It is essential that the largest single unit in the English-speaking world, the United States of America, in its tradition the heir of Locke and Jefferson, should not again weaken the international structure by pulling out of Europe or EurAsia. In a democracy indeed a large conscript or standing army, such as the U.S.S.R. or China can readily command, is always unpopular. Such an admitted authority as Marshal Zhukov can remind us that atomic weapons can launch an assault, but only infantry masses can complete a victory. As Defence Minister Emanuel Shinwell has said, the trouble with France is that she has so far followed the primrose path that she is under-manned to implement her own policies. Nevertheless, there is an immense temptation to rely upon painless-for-me defence, by push-button methods or by scientific gadgets. Unhappily this means, in contemporary terms, reliance on *Schrecklichkeit* and Terror, upon the hydrogen bomb and inter-continental missiles.

The strategy of 'Fortress America' can take this shape. Pleasing to a self-indulgent electorate—and every electorate in one aspect, having power, is self-indulgent—it can be the worst propaganda in the world. Thanks to defiance of all rules of discrimination in war, under which radio-active 'fall-outs' (as the Alsops point out) could be blown by the wind against millions of European friends, a policy could issue in which the task of the Soviet opposition in propaganda becomes a walk-over. The devil himself could not have devised a better method of making America unpopular.

It is doubtful whether anybody should be in a position to launch war who cannot expect to feel the consequences in his own skin or his children's. This is not unrecognized. Possibly as a Catholic following the moral directives of the Holy See, no other than a member of the U.S. Atomic Energy Commission, Mr. Thomas Murray, has said to the Senate Foreign Relations sub-committee that America "as a nation under God is obliged to act under the limitation of the moral law." At our present distance from the event he did not think that the use even of the atomic bomb, in the destruction of Hiroshima and its multitudes of innocent people, could be justified on moral grounds.

The continuation of further multimegaton thermonuclear tests, already clearly condemned by the Holy See, he proposed "should be stopped." "The use of force in warfare is subject to the dictates of the moral conscience." This statement must obviously be placed in the context of some system, if not of inspection then of detection, which makes infringement as dangerous as war itself, because involving it, and which makes the abstinence from such super-experiments in explosion (such as, employed in actual war, would have a boomerang effect in destruction issuing in either revolution or tyranny) to be both universal and assured.

Out of this moral imbroglio I see only one way. It is idle to suppose that, in a political situation where the restrictive Bricker Amendment commanded so much support, even although the Ball-Fulbright Resolution of Congress took an American initiative in the direction of integration, the United States of America is going to join Europe to-morrow in a political union. This means, in my view, that at the moment the lively prospects of sovereign high authorities lie in Europe. It does not mean that the vista ends there.

The stronger, economically, politically, and strategically, the European Union, the greater the pressure on North America to come in; and the informal Paris assembly of all Atlantic parliamentarians is to be here welcomed as an educational and liberal measure. Although this union may be in many respects unpleasant for the British elector, Britain must yet go along with it so far as (for example, in agriculture) she can secure Commonwealth concurrence. This is the immediate issue now.

Nevertheless, it is yet *more* important: (a) that the Commonwealth shall not be politically broken up; (b) that the pace of the six European countries involved in Euratom schemes must not be slowed to that of the fifteen countries of NATO (or the seventeen of the Organization for European Economic Cooperation), or the latter precipitously quickened to the pace of the six; (c) that the strategic scheme of 'Fortress America' shall not become merely a fine-sounding name for an actual withdrawal of the United States into a new isolation.

The three propositions connect in the sense that, whatever may be said for Lord Beaverbrook's dedicated crusading, in fact Canada and the Commonwealth cannot be more closely integrated except at a pace connived at by the United States, the geographically focal point of the bloc, and by its Senate.

Here, then, the position remains fluid and experimental, with yet the practical consequence that the United States must assume, in every concrete way and also in her announced propaganda and statements, the attitude and responsibilities of partnership, both in the United Nations forum and in the established and confident habits of Atlantic cooperation and organic union. What contributes to this, not only as a matter of fluctuating sentiment but of institutional commitment is good; and what opposes it is bad.

What the nations of the Free World, and quite especially the new nations and the small nations, require is a sense, not that they are being dictated to by arrogance or tyranny or having an outmoded doctrine thrust down their throats, but that *they are partners in a great common undertaking— and, moreover, wanted and understood partners*. The issue is psychological.

The American danger is that the American people will either abandon its sense of mission in cynicism or pursue it, as a matter of 'the American century,' in a provincial, colonial and farmer-boy spirit of telling older civilizations what their pattern of life ought to be.

The American hope is something different. Two and more

centuries ago, England (which was a new state amid the established powers of Europe, its importance something subsequent to the discovery of America) became an accepted teacher of a newly democratic Europe as a tutor in political freedom and the home of the Mother of Parliaments. The English were arrogant and often crude, but they evaded hostility and fear by a not unskilful political tactic. The great American tradition—of which President Eisenhower and Mr. Adlai Stevenson are in their respective ways exponents, not only distinguished but entirely admirable—a tradition indeed Lincolnian, needs with more self-confidence, faith and courage to be caused to shine forth with lucidity again.

The present writer has the sentiment, as an Englishman, to confess that he would be very sorry to reach the day when the noble hymn of Spring Rice or even the anthem of Elgar could not be sung without a snigger or an apology. This is no time for a retreat from greatness. The fact yet remains that power has no substitutes. There will be some, therefore, who will look back. However, when George Washington proclaimed that he was a Virginian but, first of all, an American, he did not look back. He looked forward to new actual power. Twice England has followed, or rather led, in the same process of merger and Phoenix-like expansion, when England became Great Britain and when Britain became the Commonwealth. The same process to grandeur must continue. And of the United States, if it is not to follow the deadly way of self-satisfied ossification, the same story should be told.

The day of the older sovereignties is growing to its end. The nations of men unite and the frontiers fall. Nor is this only a gospel for Europe. It is not fitting, whatever the excuse of police convenience, that America should be the land of the fingerprint, which is a slur on all in order to be a police protection of some. We can leave such markings to

Animal Farm. The issue for America is whether she is going to rise to the moral heights of her world responsibility.

And here, it is fit to conclude, the matter is not a one way street, of the United States inviting the partnership of others. It is for the free world to make clear to the American of farm and field, from the plains of Nebraska to the valleys of Shenandoah, that this world has enough respect for the great American Experiment, still in travail—that experiment upon which de Tocqueville placed such stress—to desire the partnership of the United States.

Perhaps the gravest day would be that, not only for herself but for humanity, when the United States was found to have lost confidence in herself and had ceased to be true to that for which once she stood. Let us hope that America will never be weighed in the balance and found wanting.

VII

THERE IS ANOTHER COUNTRY

1

"IF Western civilization is to save its body, it must save its soul too." The words are those of Adlai Stevenson. In his book *Is Anybody Listening?* Mr. W. H. Whyte speaks of the myth in Europe about America that "we are the New Carthage—all money and no spirit; that we are, in short, a country without a soul." This myth, he writes, cannot be discredited because "our congenital dislike of abstract thought has at last come home to roost." Maybe it is not only abstract thought, in the French and German and Marxist styles. It is just thought. Even in a land that makes a 'science' of public relations, the idea that "words can shape men's actions"—have their own magic—is merely not believed or is too embarrassing when there is no public philosophy or affirmative faith. Instead of emphasis of a positive case, at the most there is an irritated analysis of Bolshevik error. It is not enough.

England is in no better case at all. Perhaps the British Broadcasting Corporation is more respected than the Voice of America, but its bright young men are not more influential. The mood of the country is sicklied o'er by the reflection that, after two great victories and an heroic statesmanship, the country is a declining power, ironically without even the ever-springing dynamism of Germany. The Suez Canal enterprise was in part a 'declaration of independence', a desperate endeavour to assert a power that was slipping, without any constructive notion of great statesmanship about how to achieve, by the shaping of a new, wider community, the heights of new British grandeur.

133

It is Hallam Tennyson, the grandson of the great poet, (interestingly enough the follower of the Indian saint, Vinoba Bhave), who reports of his talks with all the world as, like Chaucer's pilgrims, it passed by the wayside, that "each of them had lost confidence in Britain and thought that we had come to the end of the road." They did not for a moment believe Mr. Khrushchev's bullying nonsense to the effect that Western civilization is to be equated with 'capitalism,' and capitalism with slavery. The old rich, on the contrary, were in the process of being eliminated (and much of the more sober middle class, as touching their old ways, with them) by taxation. The ordinary folk continued to believe that, in a free exchange of ideas, their standards of human dignity and decency ought to prevail. But precisely they were not pilgrims—or they were pilgrims without a shrine. The Anglo-Saxon world needs stirring up.

It is an interesting and, I believe, encouraging thought that even so marked and flamboyant an imperialist as Rudyard Kipling expressed the humble views which he did in *Recessional*. It would be less interesting were it not authentically the national spirit at its best. Likewise, surely the grand Battle Hymn of the Republic is one of the least bellicose and boastful of national hymns. Here, if anywhere, in the combination of the practical with the ideal is the Anglo-Saxon contribution to the world's civilization. And, in talking about "I vow to thee, my country," we do well to remember the last stanza of Ambassador Spring Rice's striking hymn, from which I have taken the title of this chapter. A certain shyness, American no less than British, has caused us to hesitate to communicate to the peoples of more extrovert or operatic countries that we were capable of these feelings.

2

Hitherto, in this book on a subject which could be so vast, I have endeavoured to limit myself to such things as political science can objectively discuss: to goals almost universally accepted and to the hard ways and means in practice of achieving these goals; and to the kind of ideas and persuasive propaganda which could lead vast masses of men to prefer one route or set of priorities, rather than another, towards the attainment of these goals.

We have endeavoured to disentangle and pick out certain issues, in politics, in which men's aims were so far clear and unambiguous (at least in the West, but not there only) that one could reasonably expect wide agreement about the efficient means to reach them. One such set of aims was the enforcement of the civil peace on a world scale, the elimination of violence between nations and the reign of law, in a fashion compatible with the natural rights of freedom of the person and with social justice.

Here, however, we discovered two broad proposals of means to these ends, in competition for men's trust and support: that of the Soviets, and that of the Free World. The former has small use, in its blue-prints for peace, for Natural Law or for emphasis upon personal rights; it condones police tyranny as necessary, and subordinates humanity to some yet-to-be-achieved goal of power; and it maintains, up to the present, that no route more moderate, or humane or merciful to flesh and blood, than its own can, by liquidating opposition, prepare the way for the implementation of these blue-prints.

The second set of proposals have to show how they, more than the Soviet Empire's, can remove the real evils of imperialism, imperialist colonialism, the domination of nature by nation, and arrogant customs that destroy human fraternity and the community of man. They cannot evade that challenge if they are to win the loyalty of youth. But it is possible for the Commonwealth of Free Nations to accept as a whole such a scheme as was outlined in the last chapter for international peace, in a fashion which does not spell 'a desolation' but a decent respect for personal freedom and for social justice between groups and races.

However, blue-prints of means and institutions are, philosophically, no satisfactory end to the story of human hope or to our estimates in assessing the worthwhile nature of civilisations.

In this last chapter I want, not indeed to answer, but to propose and provoke to an answer, a more difficult set of questions, questions about the nature of the Good Society. They are questions to which the answers will depend, let us admit, upon our own personal philosophy. Nor will those who get the most votes for their philosophy necessarily be the most right.

It is not my view that the answers will or should be uniform. Tolerance is too often the child of indifference or of moral pessimism, and is difficult to commend to the passionate puritan or patriot or nationalist. We have yet to put ourselves to school to distinguish obdurately between those areas where coercion by secular law is appropriate to assure the civil peace and agreed welfare, and those where all civilised advantages tie with free moral choice and the individual quest by the candle of reason and judgement.

Here the liberal West differs from Marxism. It holds that human fallibility is such, even indeed in choosing its infallibilities, that our apprehension of truth, although sometimes sure, is yet incomplete. Were the answers uniform by imposition, then history and man's adventure of ideas would come to a stop. Technology would be all—technology and its parent, matter. (Even technology has a second parent, in the inventive mind.) These answers must spring from the freely choosing, but *also* from the cultivated, mind. Their salvation must be chosen and appropriated. It is apparently the case that Professor Julian Huxley, in his Beatty Lectures, anticipates that, in the course of cultural exchange and evolution, there will be an increasing synthetic culture and the adoption of one public philosophy, which one may suspect that he would name Scientific Humanism. Of this a scientific 'clerisy' (to use Coleridge's term) would be the authoritative high priests. I am frank to confess that, while allowing for a tendency towards the unity of human judgement upon aesthetic values, this is yet not my view of development. There will be those who keep to the grand tradition, and there will be those of conventional provincial views ; there will be 'outsiders' who probe to become 'insiders' ; and there will be rebels and heresiarchs from pride and choice. All we can say is that there are diversities of gifts as touching insight with which poets and prophets, *savants* and sages and saints, are able to look into the profundities of the human spirit. But it becomes each thinker to say what his own answers are and, furthermore, to give a reason for the faith and certainties that are in him.

Moreover, we do well to note that the great movements of ideas which have swayed the history of mankind—Stoic cosmopolitanism, Christian brotherhood, Islamic puritan equalitarianism, Whig stress on natural rights and parliamentary liberties, 'the ideas of '89,' even nationalism itself— springing articulately from a few thinkers, far less in number than any one nation, have never remained as a pure national 'pattern,' but have gone on, across frontiers, to sweep a ready world.

Even in such a limited matter as the Arab Revolt of the First World War, T. E. Lawrence describes it as "rolling before the breath of an idea". Nationalism, as Mazzini emphasized, was borne on the wings of an idea. So was Christian Humanism. So will be the sacred cause of humanity, or a renascent Catholic Humanism—the cause of what Marcus Aurelius called "the dear city of God". Some are so blind that they cannot see these things. The Communist Party is here far less materialist than they. As Marshal Bulganin has said in so many words (Nov. 1956), "It is the superior ideology which will win".

On the other hand, it will be noted that no great movement in all history has been got under way by intellectual cleverness and still less by a carping negativism. We need to say this at a time when a kind of verbalism or Termism has become philosophically fashionable, beyond the proper and important requirements of exactitude of thought and respect for truth, such as has scarcely been seen since Scotus, Ockam and the late Scholastics.

At a late and transitional stage of high civilization, such as for example that of the Sophists in Greece, at a phase in the Renaissance and of the Enlightenment, we can say that its outstanding representatives were 'clever.' But not when the decisive and shaping moments were being reached was this the characteristic.

Where the critical intellect can indeed—and must—come into play, if we are not to lapse into anti-intellectualism, is in exposing, with integrity, to honesty of thought a system containing conflicting claims, distorted uses and ambiguities of terms, double-talk and inherent contradictions. Where a critical taste can come into play is in noting the startling vulgarity, by Leninist standards themselves, of such a man as the *gopak*-dancing Mr. Khrushchev. These are not the acceptable leaders of men for long.

3

To discuss the Good Society is to discuss political philosophy and ethics. In my view (which I cannot argue here) to discuss the ethical judgement is to discuss aesthetics and an objective beauty. It seems also to be the view of such a man as Wittgenstein, as it was that of Goethe. The conviction of that beauty can, to use the old Stoic phrase, "seize us by the hair of the head." It can "waylay us." But we cannot prove by any logic that this or that must be regarded as beautiful, fitting, decent. There will always be degrees of apprehension, variety of view and multiplicity of judgements, depending upon men's gifts and cultivation.

A liberal philosophy always admits this. Ethics and the philosophy of politics and society will always have to confront this. They are not sciences in Lord Kelvin's sense. They are not reducible to a humanism strictly 'natural-scientific'. This admission, moreover, must affect the shape of the desirable social order and its law. It should not affect the dynamism of individual faith swayed by reason.

There can be no one 'Public Philosophy,' equally accepted by all or imposed on them. *Oportet haereses esse.* But there can be a profound conviction that, by every standard of human experience and of inspired insight, certain things and conduct are evil and that certain are good and should prevail. In the last resort we are trusting in faith the intention of humanity and the spirit of man, to detect the right. And we are affirming that that will prevail and deserves to prevail, were it Marxism, Christianity, secular humanism or whatever, *which in fact has the genius most deeply to penetrate into the profundities of that human spirit* as it springs from reality or, as theologians would say, that spirit as it is divinely sustained—not the abnormal spirit but the profound and universal spirit. Politics and the social order are based, not as Mr. Plamenatz says, on institutions, but on the nature of man.

I have elsewhere urged that, if we wish to discover the values, indicated by reason and instinct but approved by the cultivated taste of mankind, we must turn to the pages of History. They will not prove that our direct contention is right; but they will indicate to us the great probabilities. There is, in my view, a Grand Tradition or what Professor Sir Ernest Barker chooses to call, to use the title of his book, *Traditions of Civility.* It is not our dictator in high civilization, but it is our mentor and guide.

Nor do I believe that a historiography of ideas alone, even if constructive and evaluative and not merely (as in the writing of Professor Sabine) Humean and sceptic, will provide all we need. The folk tradition and folk drama, the culture and cultus, can also help those who can read and see. Above all, this is true of the great religious dramas of mankind.

Those who stress that man is distinctively *homo faber*, having technological gifts which the ant and the bee also begin to share, sometimes forget that man is quite uniquely *homo pictor* since the days of the caves of Aurignac; and that, if these early activities connected with magic, yet later in the Eleusinian mysteries and the Greek drama in honour of the gods we find a fusion of art with the people's religion.

Some, of course, are not appealed to by such drama, just as some prefer to sit while the National Anthem is played in order to show their freedom and independence. Why Marxism wins is because Lenin and Stalin, whose ikons decorate a million Russian walls, seem to provide, for millions of believers, the best contemporary drama. It is yet my belief that it happens to be an anti-humanist, atheist or power-revering, and unhealthy drama. This is not to say that there is no hypocrisy in the West. It is to say that the traditional values which I have been discussing are indeed values, however much we may have lost a sense of their vitality.

There is a tendency, and in some qualified ways a most proper tendency, to say that the major evil in the world, to which we should practically address ourselves, is poverty. If everybody had more food, milk, housing, money, everything would be brighter. The Sicilian peasant is very poor. He should have more money. The only idea that matters for happiness is that of the domestic re-arrangement of money.

I do indeed agree that the normalization of Russia is likely to be thrust upon its rulers by the insistent demand of its too patient workers for consumption goods, which

140

its doctrinaire and fear-ridden rulers withhold as whole burnt-offerings to a metaphysical god, a Moloch State.

But the second, and not so simple, stage is reached when we note that Sicilian citric products are being driven from the markets of Europe in part because of the 'high price of labour' in Sicily. Superficially astonishing, on analysis this means that the collective cost of manpower is higher than it should be (as was found in the days of slavery in the Southern American States) compared with the cost of machines.

Collective cheap labour is not economic. So we come to the question of technology and planning, as in Russia. It is not just a question of the Italian rich man and landlord being rapacious and selfish or of the Sicilian landowner being a born gambler. It is a question of a new technical approach which is being resisted by obstinacy and indolence.

Sometimes, however, from lack of an adequate and sympathetic social perspective, that new technical approach— as was threatened in Burma, with American recommendations to convert a rural into an industrial civilization overnight—can get out of hand. Nothing is more un-human than the cult of efficiency. Should we, indeed, in the name of efficiency and progress, so as to have, 'some day', more money to distribute, push change through by purges in which millions perish, as in the Ukraine, and by the massive use of efficient power? Or does the preservation of life and respect for the rights of others matter the less, because we recognize that social controls securing the needs of the full stomach also matter to man?

The Twentieth Century is peculiarly characterized by its desire to kiss power, any power. It shares this characteristic with the shadier aspects of the Renaissance. The Victorian Age was marked by an uneasy but dynamic combination (which has lasted longer in America) of respect for money together with a certain Puritanism of the scribes and lawyers.

In Western Europe, under the impact of two wars, the scene has shifted. We are invited, even in the British Conservative press, to look up to Stalin because, for all his atrocities of which we have heard, he was very powerful. Hitler, in throwing off the shackles of Versailles that were offensive to the pride of his nation, was also very powerful. No character in history rose from so obscure to so powerful a position, from being the young dreamer of Linz in the poor home to being the dictator of Europe, in so short a time. But Stalin was even more blessed by 'the bitch goddess,' Success . . . Let us then worship. Or ourselves cultivate success even more busily . . .

As Hallam Tennyson says of Britain, there is in a democracy not only a question of keeping up with the Jones but also of pleasing the Joneses, of conforming to the local *mores*, of conforming 'to the party line' as Republicans or Democrats, or of doing nothing to damage our prospects of success with the neighbourhood. Granted full employment and the abolition of the nightmare of the empty stomach, then it comes to be this 'success' that is what matters. So we shall enjoy the little power that is all that can be got into our pintpot . . . Is this—first material sufficiency, then appetite for personal success—enough?

The science of politics is largely the study of power. The issues of economics, when we come to the ordering of society, pass over into issues of what kind of society we will be prepared to support, pay the costs to support; and into issues of power. And here the nature of our good society will be shaped by our mental attitude to power. If this is our 'philosophy' or a judgement of what is fitting, then our problem is one of our public philosophy. After most of a lifetime spent in the study of power I am convinced that, as we pass from means to the realm of ends, much of our concern in answering the enigma of power is, as touching domination, to transcend and go out beyond it. It is to put national and personal 'success' in perspective. But how?

The sceptic Hume held that the answers to our social problems lay in institutions, and in habits formed by institutions. In the last chapter I have given full measure to what I believe that international and domestic institutions can do. However, in several of his recent books Bertrand Russell has repeated that the answer to our problems of peace, freedom and justice—and indeed our answer to boredom and sense of emptiness and frightened loneliness—lies also in education behind habits, and lies *within* as the possibility of change in the spirit of man—not change contrary to his nature but in change transforming and enlightening his nature. I believe Russell to be right. The fault lies not in our stars or in some cosmic dialectic. The operation of the Logos, the Word, is by grace. And the fault lies in ourselves.

The task is *not* to discard institutional change in favour of individual reform, but to give dynamism in institutional and social change here on earth, *sicut in coelo et in terra ;* as Plato said, by a convinced vision of spirit, by a new insight.

3

Power is usually associated with domination. The obsessive desire for domination arises from distrust. Manchester capitalist and Marx-Leninist have agreed on that distrust. The new insight, confirmed by the newer scientific psychology, rests on trust. *And on a precise educational discipline in rational trust.*

It is easy to talk in facile fashion about cooperation. But cooperation about what? Surely not in cooperation in pleasing the Joneses, whatever their opinions; or in conforming to the dictates of a picayune and provincial culture which is almost the enemy and precise antithesis of a catholic culture of religious humanism, seeking to be as wide as an articulate humanity and as profound as the human spirit, plumbed by genius. There must be a principle.

I have commented that there are certain strains in American intellectual thought, which especially plumes itself on being 'democratic,' that end by affirming that all opinions are equal, each as entitled to be thought valid, 'because it is mine,' as another. It ends in a moral nihilism which (like all nihilism) finishes with the rule of force in the shape of mundane success and of a cheap and cynical commercialism or money-power. Most can see that this is an abomination; but not all are honest in admitting why it has come to be.

Plato set, over against opinion, knowledge. And, at his most profound, he asserted that guidance, to seekers in what was in this context knowledge, must be attributed to those whom he compared to master musicians. All have the gift in divers measures to see the beautiful; but they, the master musicians, are those competent for our education in taste. It has been for the churches at their best to insist that this guidance to the good must be freely chosen by the individual of conscience, conscientiously seeking enlightenment, wider than any local Bethel; and that this good is of a kind of *social order* of the communion, a beauty expressed through symbols perhaps in a mystery, but still in a *public* mystery or presentation or evangel, and not to a few elect or to clever initiates.

Bluntly, what we require is not a new imposed Public Philosophy, but a public drama to capture men's whole souls better than Hegelian Marxism has done. Its theme must be to proclaim the dignity of man and its problem to manifest in what that dignity consists. It is not necessary that vast masses should be converted or convinced. Most of the great changes of the world have been wrought by a dedicated few. The Quakers, who have contributed so much recently that is respectworthy, are few. It is sufficient that enough are convinced.

It is interesting on the record, it is interesting as a sociological fact, that the most persistent and dedicated resistance

144

to Leninist Communism, from Poland to Indo-China has been offered by Catholicism, and one great strength of Catholicism lies in its catholicism. According to Communist 'self-criticism', Catholic dedication has exceeded that of the Party members.

The Church is of course a vast mass body of about a seventh of humanity. Hegelianism as a philosophy may be dead but, at least, it can teach us that no such mass body can, or even should be, without dust and spot and dis-figurement, or without the contamination of power. But the Catholicism to which I here refer is not a dead Christianity but that of thousands of dedicated if sinning humble folk— a style of life more abundant, more possessed of shape, more 'worthwhile' than the trivial. And it is important ever to remember that Communists also are human beings, even idealists, capable of reason, with souls to be saved, not incapable of goodwill and able to be impressed and converted.

There is not, I think, any mystery in all this. What is required is not the unity of Christendom but the union in practical matters of all sincere religious men, concerned with human dignity as "above the level of dogs and rats." It is a theme touched upon by that remarkable man, Russell Davenport, in his book *The Dignity of Man*. Here is to be found the new drama which is yet old. There will be some who will derive their inspiration from a Vinoba Bhave or a Mohandas Gandhi.

The present writer recalls with gratitude that it was the Mahatma who told him that one did not have to aspire to great responsibilities and successes in order to find that which could make life worthwhile; that what one should do always lay to one's hand, springing from oneself. There will be those who derive inspiration from Albert Schweizer and are here prepared to see a virtue in 'commitment.' I have no illusion at all that peculiarly the Anglo-Saxon world will become Catholic, or more explicitly Christian,

145

overnight ; nor do I think it at all good that it should adopt any mechanical uniformity, anticipating the slow, persuasive uniformity dictated by reason and taste—although a reasoned and grave commitment is good. My argument is different but yet contains, I believe, a truth that should be accepted.

It was the Rabbi of Akiba, in the Second Century, who said that the Song of Songs had no less the value of canonical Scripture than the Torah itself. It was Sholem Asch who, to a Jewish orthodox gathering, recently said that the music of Beethoven and the paintings of Rembrandt were also part of the Law. In one diffused sense of secularist humanism this is very wrong and mere *Kultur*. In the sense intended, that man worships God in all his highest works, as some have by dancing, it is deeply true. In what has been called 'the solemn pavan' of the Mass, God is worshipped; and there is declared gloriously His glory, *quoniam elevata est magnificentia Tua super coelos* (*Gradual of the Ninth after Pentecost*), "because Thy magnificence is elevated above the Heavens." There is, to use technical language, 'a sense of the holy' and what also Herbert Read calls 'the sense of glory.' These human duties, pains, courage and dedication are put into the proportion of the worthwhile—not on the basis of domination which springs from fear, but of a power, charity and principle which can cast out fear by trust. There is a glorification of divine power and a putting into perspective of the quarrelsome ambitions of men. It is the solution in trust of the sphinx question of the ages, the enigma of the moral value or evil of power.

This dynamic of faith has one especial virtue. It makes plain goodness in the human fraternity, the goodness that poets have seen in peasants, the goodness of any common man doing his duty—it makes this goodness important. It provides an almost naive gospel of the Good Man. Not only success—which in so many cases is a deadly foe to the sense of duty and honour. Not only domination.

Nor party metaphysic. What we are arguing, and not naively, is that every average man is able to judge that something which we call 'a good man'; to judge him by the beauty of his life. That is the direct aesthetic judgement. That is the central ethical judgement. And we should not be ashamed of it or seek to sophisticate it. By the fruits in the life of such a man we can judge how our own lives may be worthwhile, and how we shall be able to enliven quotidian duties. And I submit that the clue to these lives lies not in the lust for dominative power and success, but in a trust vindicated by experience. 'Shape,' elegance and rich culture may also matter, but they yet matter less.

I would even hazard the suggestion that such men also succeed by a gift peculiarly important in human relations, a gift of detachedly projecting themselves into the position of the other man and of asking how would they behave were they he. "Manners maketh man." From this springs treatment with understanding, not strifes, massacres and liquidations watering with blood the field for new hates, rivalries, liquidations, such as is amply documented on the historic record.

Moreover a very few good men can achieve great changes if they have persistence. Politics rests upon a few people having a strong sense of responsibility—and commanding the support of many. And without such men the finest paper institutions grow corrupt in practice, fail in effect and perish.

Is the conclusion of the whole matter: Be good? I do not think so. It is not so simple at all. Is it: Have trust; believe in the possibility of change; be patient to understand your fellow man? 'It is not who's right but what's right.' That may be means to it, if we understand that this is not a slogan but a conclusion in analytical psychology. Is it: Be a mystic? Or be a prophet? Is this the truth? This comes nearer to the vision transcending analysis and negating the distrustful appetite for power, the neurotic fear, the inculcated distrust, of which I speak.

Fear is very nearly the final enemy; and it requires, not mere counter-fear, but *courage* and also education in charity to meet it, an education which effects (as Gandhi in his *ashram* sought to effect; as St. Benedict in his 'workshops of souls' sought to effect) psychological training and change.

What I am really saying is that, discussing goals and here leaving politics behind, we are in quest of the worthwhile and significant. We are in quest of the light that blazes in life, beyond the 'one-damned-thing-after-another-ness' of living. There are limited practical goals to which almost all men aspire and others with which political parties are properly concerned.

There are the obvious goods of civil peace. There is the chaffering of the political market between liberty and security. But, in the last resort, not only men but nations— and here Soviet Russia is no exception—live by something else. Sometimes their living faith and conviction is rational and concordant with men's long established judgement of what does not disappoint; sometimes for a while it is twisted and concerned with some local or class victory which will end by being seen for what it is, as a local or class one, selfish and, because selfish, narrow and because narrow, cheap and unsatisfying. For a while there is the warm human satisfaction of marching together, rank on rank, in a mass for a cause: and then it passes. Against this it is precisely true that men find satisfaction in a vision high and lifted up, human and more than merely human, of which what the Jews called the *shekinah*, the beauty and glory, can give satisfaction to their lives.

The *shekinah* will be found in many places, although in some more than others. At this level we find the solution to the enigma of power. It may be true that, in Napoleon's words, mere power, which can be vulgar, yet is "never ridiculous." Nevertheless, in this realm of ends, we yet find that power can at last separate off from lust for domination. There is an inescapable appreciation of that which has power to command, which is unconnected with immediate advantages and unrelated to calculations of distrust. Even that present fear of violent death which the philosopher Hobbes alleged was man's major motivation loses obsessive power and courage is born anew.

The wind and the spirit blow whither they list. No man can say that we know that the vitalizing spirit will be seen or not seen in East or West. The task is to follow without fear where it burns most brightly. It is, in the judgement of this writer, to be found in the Franciscan Missions of California and in the council chambers of Delhi and also 'in England's green and pleasant land.' It is expressed in the great treasure of Helleno-Judaic culture but also in the poetry of T'ang. Some indeed would just call it high civilization and its devotees the humanists. To be permitted, allowed, privileged to contribute to this we may say is what the West really wants—but Goethe and also Dante will tell is that the drama of human life is more than 'Western.'

Some, such as Mr. E. M. Forster, rather turn their attention to the bearers of these values, to a kind of aristocratic tradition of humane integrity, to a humanistic brotherhood. It is yet (and here early Communists were right as were some church saints) easily suffocated by too much sophistication.

For myself, it seems to me that what we have here is more than just humanism, but rather something that streams from an objective beauty, which St. John calls "the Father of Lights," and which is no more the same as secular humanism than the writing of verses is the same as the voices that spoke to Saint Joan of Domrémy.

What the West wants, and not the West alone, is a Saint Joan. "Moreover by the means of her I shall have immor-

149

tality: and shall leave behind me an everlasting memory unto them that come after me"—(*Wisdom*, viii, being the Epistle for her saint's day). The West has suffered from spiritual deadness. Perhaps it will not remain dead.